Scotland
Highlands
and Islands

AA Publishing

Authors: John Baxter, David Winpenny, Pat and Charles Aithie

Original photography: Jim Henderson

Page layout: Stuart Perry

Produced by AA Publishing

Published by AA Publishing (a trading name of Automobile Association Developments Limited, whose registered office is Millstream, Maidenhead Road, Windsor, Berkshire, SL4 5GD. Registered Number 1878835)

First edition published 1996, reprinted 1996, 1997, 1998. Second edition 1999, reprinted 2000 Third edition 2002.

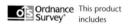 Ordnance Survey® This product includes mapping data licensed from Ordnance Survey® with the permission of the Controller of Her Majesty's Stationery Office.
© Crown copyright 2002. All rights reserved. Licence number 399221

Mapping produced by the Cartographic Department of The Automobile Association. A00691.

ISBN 07495 3299 8

A CIP catalogue record for this book is available from the British Library.

Gazetteer map references are taken from the National Grid and can be used in conjunction with Ordnance Survey maps and atlases. Places featured in this guide will not necessarily be found on the maps at the back of the book.

All the walks are on rights of way, permissive paths or on routes where de facto access for walkers is accepted. On routes which are not on legal rights of way, but where access for walkers is allowed by local agreements, no implication of a right of way is intended.

The contents of this book are believed correct at the time of printing. Nevertheless, the publishers cannot accept responsibility for errors or omissions, or for changes in details given in this guide or for the consequences of any reliance on the information it provides. We have tried to ensure accuracy in this book, but things do change and we would be grateful if readers would advise us of any inaccuracies they may encounter.

Visit the AA Publishing website at www.theAA.com

Colour reproduction by L C Repro

Printed and bound by G. Canale & C. s.p.a., Torino, Italy

Contents

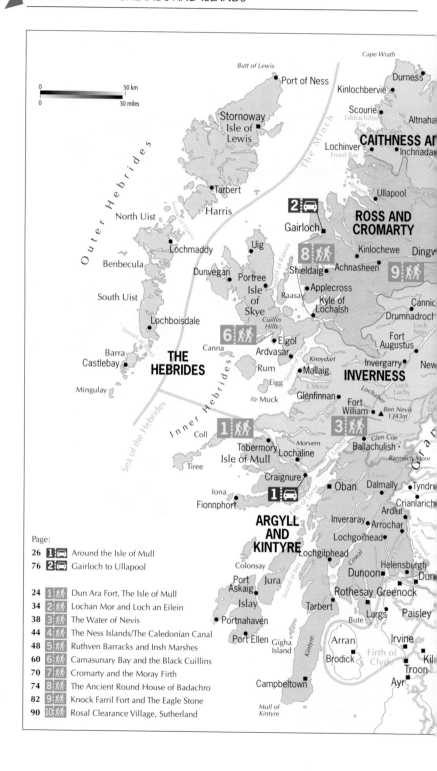

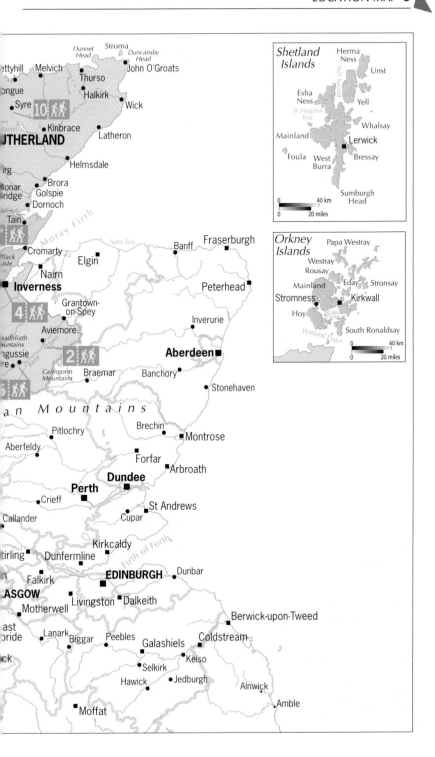

ettyhill • Melvich
ongue
• Syre **10** 🚶🚶
UTHERLAND
Javern
irg
Sonar
bridge
• Tain
🚶🚶

Dunnet Head
Stroma
Duncansby Head
John O'Groats
• Thurso
• Halkirk
• Wick
• Kinbrace
• Latheron
• Helmsdale
• Brora
Golspie
• Dornoch
Moray Firth
• Cromarty
Black Isle
Spey Bay
Banff
• Elgin
Nairn
Inverness
Grantown-on-Spey
4 🚶🚶
Aviemore
nadhliath untains
ngussie
re
River Spey
2 🚶🚶
Cairngorm Mountains
Braemar
Banchory
Fraserburgh
• Peterhead
• Inverurie
Aberdeen ■
• Stonehaven

an **M o u n t a i n s**
• Pitlochry
Aberfeldy
Brechin
■ Montrose
• Forfar
Dundee
■ Arbroath
Perth
• Crieff
St Andrews
Callander
Cupar
Kirkcaldy
tirling ■
Dunfermline
Firth of Forth
Falkirk
EDINBURGH
• Dunbar
ASGOW
Livingston ■ Dalkeith
• Motherwell
ast oride
• Lanark Biggar
Peebles
Galashiels
Coldstream
Berwick-upon-Tweed
ck
• Selkirk
• Kelso
Hawick
• Jedburgh
Alnwick
• Amble
• Moffat

Shetland Islands

Herma Ness
Esha Ness
Unst
St Magnus Bay
Yell
Yell Sound
Whalsay
Mainland
Foula
West Burra
■ Lerwick
Bressay
Sumburgh Head

0 — 40 km
0 — 20 miles

Orkney Islands

Papa Westray
Westray
Rousay
Eday
Stronsay
Mainland
Stromness
■ Kirkwall
Hoy
Scapa Flow
Pentland Firth
South Ronaldsay

0 — 40 km
0 — 20 miles

Introducing The Scottish Highlands and Islands

One of the last truly unspoilt areas of Europe, the Highlands and Islands cover about half of Scotland. The Highlands are probably most famous for their dramatic and colourful landscape – the Cairngorms, Glencoe, and the Nevis Range; more unexpected, perhaps, are the gardens of the west coast, where palm trees and exotic flowering shrubs flourish, warmed by the Gulf Stream. Sheltered sandy beaches are surprisingly frequent, not least on the extraordinarily beautiful islands of Harris and Barra.

Britain's largest mammal, the red deer, forages in the Highlands, beneath the eye of the eagle; there are hides from which to view ospreys, and dolphins abound in the Moray Firth. Vast lochs and majestic rivers are home to the best salmon and trout.

OSPREY
Above, ospreys, hunted almost to extinction, returned to Scotland in 1955 and may be seen in summer at the RSPB's Loch Garten reserve

HAGGIS
Haggis (left) with potato and 'bashed neeps' is the traditional dish; haggis and chips is widely available

CALLANISH STANDING STONES
The Highlands have a legacy of mysterious standing stones and prehistoric monuments, none finer than the stone circle of Callanish on Lewis, above

WOOLLEN MILL
As souvenirs of Scotland go, you can't do much better than a thick tartan rug – picnic on it on a sunny brae, or wrap up warm on a chilly Highland night

NESSIE
Left, the Loch Ness Monster has been avoiding unwanted attention for years

PANNING FOR GOLD
Helmsdale once had its very own gold rush, and you may still find flecks of gold in Highland streams

REINDEER
Right, reindeer at the Cairngorm Reindeer Centre near Aviemore lead a busy life, talking to summer tourists and doubling for Rudolph at Christmas

WHISKY
Left, for a drop of really fine whisky, the Highland malts take a lot of beating – judge for yourself on the Strathspey Whisky Trail

TEN BEST BOAT TRIPS
Moray Firth
Kylerhea ferry
Loch Coruisk
Loch Ness
Uig ferry
Unst ferry
Small Isles
Corran ferry
Kyles of Bute
Loch Lomond

AN ORKNEY CHAIR
Left, canny Orkney weavers developed a draught-proof chair – one of the exhibits at Kirbister farm museum

BONNIE PRINCE CHARLIE
Highland history is shot through with the Jacobite uprising of 1745 and its grim aftermath, tied in with the thwarted ambitions of the romantic and charismatic Prince Charles Edward Stuart

SHEEP ON THE ROAD
On the narrow roads of northern Scotland, sheep treat the road with a certain carelessness, so beware!

A GREAT POINT OF VIEW
Walkers stop to enjoy breathtaking views from Bidean nam Bian above Glen Coe, right

THE ESSENCE OF THE SCOTTISH HIGHLANDS AND ISLANDS

If you have little time and want to sample the essence of the Highlands and Islands:

Enjoy the romantic beauty of Eilean Donan Castle on Loch Duich, and charming Plockton... **Watch** the sun setting over the western isles... **Take** the little Mull and West Highland Narrow Gauge Railway to the delightful Torosay Castle... **Enjoy** the peace of the Iona Community... **Hop** on a ferry to the Small Isles or the Summer Isles, or go whale and dolphin watching... **Indulge** yourself at the Loch Fyne Oyster Bar... **Drive** up the pass of Bealach-na-Ba, or take the Aviemore ski-lift for spectacular views... **Take** in the history of whaling and fishing at Orkney's Stromness Museum... **Feel** on the edge of the world at Duncansby Head or Cape Wrath... **Follow** the trail of Bonnie Prince Charlie to Glenfinnan and Culloden, then back again to Skye and the Outer Hebrides... **Admire** the gardens at Inverewe and the wilderness of Assynt.

A Weekend in The Scottish Highlands and Islands: Day One

For many of us a weekend is the most that can be managed as a break in busy lives. These four pages offer an itinerary designed to ensure that you see and enjoy the very best of the Scottish Highlands, including a trip to Skye. Places within the gazetteer are in **bold**.

Friday Night

Make your way to the **Isle of Skye** and stay, if you can, at Kinloch Lodge, Lord and Lady Macdonald's secluded Edwardian lodge near Isle Ornsay. It is mainly the food which draws people here. Cookery writer Lady Macdonald uses only the best Scottish produce for her sumptuous dinners, taken in the elegant dining room under the watchful gaze of the family portraits.

There is plenty of alternative accommodation on Skye, but much of it, including Kinloch Lodge, closes down in winter, so check in advance.

Saturday Morning

Drive north on the A851 to Broadford, then turn left on to the B8083 and follow this minor road down to Elgol for wonderful scenery all along the way. Return the same way to Broadford, turn left and take the A87 north, turning left on to the A863 beyond Sconser. Follow this winding route up the west coast, turning left at Kilmuir on to the B884 for Colbost.

Enjoy breath-taking views of the Cuillins, above

Left: At Sligachan take the road west across the neck of Skye

Below, pause for refreshment at the popular Sligachan Hotel

Fortify yourself with traditional Scottish fare, right

Explore the attractions of Dunvegan Castle, below

Saturday Lunch

The Three Chimneys restaurant at Colbost is in a remote and beautiful corner of Skye, overlooking Loch Dunvegan. Within this converted crofter's cottage you can enjoy well-cooked food based on good local ingredients. The lunchtime menu includes some traditional Scottish dishes.

Saturday Afternoon

If there is time, have a look at the Black House Folk Museum at Colbost before driving back to Kilmuir and turning left for Dunvegan. Dunvegan Castle has been the seat of the MacLeod clan chiefs for nearly 800 years. The family history can be traced from its Norse origins to the present day through relics, books, pictures, arms – and don't miss the legendary Fairy Flag.

Try to fit in one of the boat trips to see brown seals at close range, basking on the skerries in front of the castle.

Saturday Night

From Dunvegan drive across the island to Kyleakin and cross the road bridge to Kyle of Lochalsh on the mainland.

Drive north east for about 5 miles (8km) to the picture-postcard village of Plockton and stay at the enchanting Haven Hotel, where you will be pampered with fine food and accommodation of a very high standard.

Seek out the delights of palm-fringed Plockton, right

A Weekend in the Scottish Highlands and Islands: Day Two

Our second day is spent back on the mainland, venturing northwards through Glenshieldaig Forest, along Loch Torridon and Loch Maree and on to visit one of the most famous gardens in the country.

Sunday Morning

From Plockton, drive east through Achmore to join the A890, turning left to drive through Stromeferry and along the southern shore of Loch Carron.

Around the head of the loch, turn left on to the A896 and follow this road back along the north shore, before turning inland and heading north across the Applecross peninsula, through Glenshieldaig Forest and on to **Torridon**.

Here, amidst some of Scotland's finest mountain scenery, is the excellent Countryside Centre. It isn't open until the afternoon, but you can stop to look at the deer museum and to view the herd of red deer kept on the estate.

Drive on up Glen Torridon, turning left on to the A832 and continuing along the shores of Loch Maree before reaching **Gairloch**.

Pass through the exquisite scenery of Loch Carron, left

Visit the Countryside Centre at Torridon, below

Bottom, follow in Queen Victoria's footsteps by Loch Maree

Sunday Lunch

Stop at The Old Inn in Gairloch for lunch. It is a former coaching inn overlooking the fishing harbour and has real ales and a good range of food.

Don't worry if your morning has been more leisurely than intended – food is available all day at the Old Inn's bistro.

Sunday Afternoon

It is only a short distance from Gairloch to Poolewe, where **Inverewe Garden** is renowned for its sub-tropical plants, which flourish in the Atlantic Drift climate. The garden is at its best in early June, but there is great beauty here at any time between March and October.

Sunday Night

A weekend in such a remote part of north-west Scotland will need a third overnight stay before you head for home.

Retrace your route back down Loch Maree to Kinlochewe, then carry straight on to Achnasheen. Here you will find Ledgowan Lodge, a delightfully friendly country house hotel in wooded grounds.

From here it is an easy drive eastwards to **Inverness,** or you can take a more convoluted route south-west towards **Fort William**. A direct route due south is, unfortunately, not an option.

Take in lunch at Gairloch, top, before going on to visit the extraordinary garden of Inverewe, above

Right, enjoy a last view of Slioch, on Loch Maree, before heading homewards

Argyll and Kintyre

Easily accessible from Glasgow, the peninsulas and islands of Argyll spill west and south from the Clyde, with the sea a constant presence. Here the many faces of Scotland come together – rugged mountains and sparkling lochs, fertile farmland and forest, busy fishing villages and remote cottages. The past is ever-present too, with prehistoric remains all around and the cradle of Celtic Christianity on the island of Iona. All of these attractions are linked by roads through high passes and by ferries that shuttle across sometimes choppy straits.

DOWN IN THE FOREST

Argyll Forest Park has stretches of open moorland and bare mountain tops as well as trees. Where conifer planting has taken place, you can still find pockets of ancient woodland, like that near Glenbranter, or more exotic species like the Tasmanian eucalyptus trees at Kilmun, the result of Forestry Commission experiments. The 53,630 acres (21,720ha) of the Park produce 70,000 tonnes of timber each year, mostly for paper and saw mills in Scotland. The forest is home to varied wildlife – only the luckiest visitor will see a golden eagle or a wildcat, but buzzards and sparrowhawks are easier to spot, and you may get a glimpse of deer, foxes or even the rare red squirrel.

The long blue finger of Loch Eck lies at the heart of the Argyll Forest Park

ARGYLL FOREST PARK Argyll & Bute

The towering, pine-clad mountains, deep valleys and narrow lochs of the Argyll Forest Park, established more than 60 years ago, are a perfect introduction to the area. You can reach the heart of the Park up Glen Croe, with the 'Arrocher Alps' to the north, of which Ben Arthur, 'The Cobbler', is the most distinctive peak. From Rest-and-be-Thankful an exciting single-track road descends Hell's Glen to Lochgoilhead, from where there are waymarked walks, including one to Rob Roy's Cave. Further down Loch Goil are the impressive remains of Carrick Castle, a 15th-century tower house.

Mountain-bikers should head for Ardgartan and Glenbranter, where they will find signed mountain-bike trails. The latter is also the start point of the delightful Lauder Forest Walks (music-hall entertainer Sir Harry Lauder once owned the land), which go through old oak woodland and rare rhododendrons to a series of

waterfalls. The best-known of the trails is up Puck's Glen, at the foot of Lock Eck, crossing many bridges through a steep, tree-lined gorge. It originally led to a folly built by the Youngers of Benmore, whose estate is now the Younger Botanic Garden. This outpost of Edinburgh's Royal Botanic Garden has high rainfall and a mild climate – ideal conditions for growing rhododendrons. There are more than 650 different types here, which make a visit in early summer a spectacular treat, but there is interest throughout the season, with conifers of all types, and paths that zigzag up the mountainside to spectacular viewpoints. Most famous of all is the avenue of redwoods, planted in 1863 – the trees are now more than 100 feet (30.5m) tall.

BUTE Argyll & Bute

Bute has been the holiday playground for generations of Glaswegians, most of whom have arrived at Rothesay on the ferry from Wemyss Bay. Finely set on the Firth of Clyde, Rothesay has a late 19th-century atmosphere created by its solid, mostly Victorian houses and decorative Winter Gardens, but much more ancient are the impressive ruins of the moated 13th-century Rothesay Castle.

The island largely consists of green and fertile hills, with superb views across the narrow Kyles of Bute to the mainland and to mountainous Arran – Ettrick Bay has an especially beautiful aspect. Further down the west coast are the ruins of a 6th-century chapel, overlooking Inchmarnock Island, while in the more mountainous area south of Bute is the mainly 12th-century St Blane's Chapel, set in a bowl of rocks on the site of a Celtic monastery. Just off the road up the east coast is one of Bute's hidden gems, the extraordinary Victorian Gothic Mount Stuart House, surrounded by gardens that lead down to the shore.

THE ULTIMATE CONVENIENCE

Since 1899 the needs of gentlemen visiting Rothesay Pier have been met in a modest building which hides a spectacular interior. Go through the etched glass door and you are in a temple of cloacal magnificence. Fourteen stalls, of white enamel, surrounded with sea-green imitation marble, stand along the wall, while six more form a central feature. The nine cubicles retain their panelled doors and wooden seats, and there is well-polished copper piping and gleaming embossed tile-work everywhere. Fittings were supplied at the cost of £530 by Twyfords of Glasgow; recent restoration cost nearly £30,000, and makes the modest entrance fee a bargain. Only the boldest ladies can see this splendour; the Victorians made no provision for them, and their adjoining facility is modern.

The royal burgh of Rothesay, Bute

Small craft shelter in the canal basin at Crinan

PARA AND THE PUFFERS
Para Handy, captain of the 'puffer' *Vital Spark*, first made his appearance in the *Glasgow Evening News* in 1905. Neil Munro's stories, set during the early 1900s, have been enjoyed by readers – and television viewers – ever since. The Crinan Canal and Loch Fyne are the heart of Para Handy country, with comic forays to Campbeltown, Mull, Arran, and frequently to Glasgow. *Vital Spark* was one of the largest of three kinds of puffers – steam-driven vessels, that get their name from the puffing noise made by the engine exhaust venting through the funnel.

CRINAN CANAL   Argyll & Bute

In 1847 Queen Victoria and Prince Albert sailed the 9 miles (14.5km) of the Crinan Canal aboard the barge *Sunbeam* – a journey used later in the century by MacBrayne's steamers to sell 'Royal Route' excursions from Glasgow to Oban. Today you are most likely to see pleasure craft negotiating the canal's 15 locks, but its purpose was to enable merchant traffic to and from the Western Isles to avoid the voyage around the Mull of Kintyre. Two famous engineers worked on the Crinan Canal, which opened in 1801. Rennie did the original engineering work, and Telford solved problems with the water supply.

From the basin at Ardrishaig, where it leaves Loch Fyne, the canal hugs the wooded hillsides as it winds up to its highest point of 64 feet (19.4m). On the hills above Cairnbaan are reservoirs that constantly replenish the water in the canal as it descends under the unusual hand-wound rolling bridge at Dunadry. Beyond here the landscape opens out into the flat marshland of the River Add estuary and then into Loch Crinan. The canal ends at the picturesque Crinan Harbour, with beautiful views over the Sound of Jura. With luck you may find a 'puffer' in the harbour to remind you of the canal's past glories.

DUNOON Argyll & Bute Map ref NS1776
Paddle steamers used to bring huge crowds from
Gourock to Dunoon, and there are still regular ferry
services here. On the grassy headland between the
town's two bays are the remains of the 13th-century
royal castle, largely destroyed in 1685. Below is the 1896
statue of Burns's love, Highland Mary, erected to mark
the centenary of the poet's death. Dunoon is busiest in
late August for the Cowal Highland Gathering, when
more than 150 pipe bands from all over the world
compete for prestigious trophies.

Morag's Fairy Glen, off the road south from Dunoon,
has shaded walks along the Berry Burn, but for more
expansive views, continue to Toward Point lighthouse
(not open) at the southern end of the A815, where you
can look out across the water to Bute and down to Largs.
In the grounds of the 19th-century Castle Toward, now
an education centre, is a ruined 15th-century tower
house, somewhat confusingly called Toward Castle. One
of the worst atrocities of the Civil War began here, when
Campbell of Ardkinglas besieged the Lamonts, who were
Stuart loyalists. Although guaranteed safety, 36 Lamont
men were taken to Dunoon and hanged – a monument
in Tom-a-Mhoid Road marks the place.

Just north of Dunoon at Lochan Wood is the attractive
Cowal Bird Garden, and this area is rich in ancient sites.
Near Sandbank, on the shore of Holy Loch, are the huge
stones forming Adam's Grave, a Neolithic burial
chamber, and you can follow a trail from near Ardnadam
Farm to see ancient field boundaries and the site of a
prehistoric enclosure.

ON THE OCEAN WAVERLEY
The world's last sea-going
paddle streamer, *Waverley*, is a
regular visitor to Dunoon and
other ports along the Clyde
coast. Launched on the Clyde
in 1947 and in service until
1973, she was bought for just
£1 by the Paddle Steamer
Preservation Society.
Following restoration, she
now regularly plies to and fro
across the Clyde during the
summer, carrying up to 950
passengers. *Waverley*, with its
two distinctive black, red and
white funnels, is 240 feet
(73.2m) long and 57 feet
(17.4m) broad across the
paddle wheels, which are 14
feet (4.2m) in diameter.
Powered by a 2,100-
horsepower steam engine, the
vessel is a welcome and
impressive sight wherever she
goes – and that has included
four trips around the whole of
Great Britain.

*Genteel pleasure gardens
adorn the front at Dunoon*

CAILEIN MOR

The Dukes of Argyll are descended from the 12th-century Colin Campbell of Loch Awe, known as Cailein Mor – Great Colin. All his successors as clan chief have been designated MacCailein Mor – Great Colin's Son, and they became successively Earls, Marquesses and Dukes of Argyll. The 1st Marquess hedged his bets in the Civil War, crowning Charles II at his Scottish coronation in 1651, but subsequently supporting Cromwell. He and his son were executed for treason at the Restoration, but by the end of the century the 11th Earl was supporting William and Mary, and the dukedom was his reward. The Dukes are Hereditary Great Masters of the Household in Scotland and their baton of office, topped with a royal Scottish lion, is on display in the castle.

Splendid slatey-blue pepperpot towers adorn Inveraray Castle

INVERARAY Argyll & Bute Map ref NN0908

Inveraray, on the shores of Loch Fyne, is as fine an example of town planning as you will find, created by the 3rd Duke of Argyll in the 1740s to sit at the gates of his grand new home. It seems an incredible amount of trouble to go to, just to move your ancestral home by half a mile (0.8km), but this was, after all, the extravagant 18th century. The little town that he created is stylish, with a wide main street of white-painted houses running up to the classical kirk. On the waterfront are brilliant white arches, one of which leads to All Saints Episcopal Church – climb the bell-tower for a wonderful panoramic view of the town, the castle, the loch and the hills.

Inveraray Castle, now home to the 12th Duke and his family, is a neo-Gothic building with pointed sash windows and battlements. Inside, its most spectacular feature is the Armoury Hall, the tallest room in Scotland, which is dramatically adorned with pikes, axes, swords and muskets. A tour of the castle includes splendid state rooms with ornate gilded plasterwork, fine furniture and Campbell family portraits.

Moored on the loch side is the three-masted vessel *Arctic Penguin*, upon which you can take a turn at steering, ring the ship's telegraph, visit the engine room and watch archive film of old sailing and steam ships. Inveraray Jail, near the kirk, has thrown open its doors to more willing visitors. In the semi-circular courtroom you can be part of the crowd hearing a trial, and in the 19th-century cells you can try out canvas hammocks and turn the crank machine. You can even see mug-shots of some of the last petty criminals to use the exercise gallery.

ISLAY, JURA, COLONSAY, SCARBA AND GIGHA

Each of these islands on the eastern side of the Minch has its own distinctive character. Jura is one of the last remaining areas of true wilderness and is dominated by the three rounded, conical peaks – The Paps of Jura; the highest, Beinn an Oir, rises to 2,572 feet (784m). Neolithic standing stones and cairns here date back to 7000 BC. Colonsay and Oronsay have their ancient monuments too, and on their west coasts are great expanses of clean sand, none better than at Kiloran Bay.

Islay is also a very special place, with remote and spectacular coastal scenery, superb hill walking and a distinctive peaty flavour to the 'water of life' distilled here. The island was once the home of the Lords of the Isles, who ruled most of the Western Isles during the 14th and 15th centuries. Loch Finlaggan was their cultural and administrative capital, its two islands originally linked by a causeway. This is one of Scotland's most important archaeological sites, with the remains of 28 buildings and an excellent interpretative centre.

Gigha, east of Islay, is the home of the Ogham Stone, with its indecipherable inscription, which was brought from Ireland in pre-Christian times, and there are plenty of standing stones – those at Kilchattan have been endowed with the wonderful name of Fingal's Limpet Hammers. The beautiful gardens at Achamore House (National Trust for Scotland) are especially noted for their dazzling displays of azaleas and rhododendrons.

Scarba, remote and uninhabited, is a small island off the northern tip of Jura, its highest point 1,470 feet (448m). It is separated from its larger neighbour by one of the most treacherous pieces of water in the world – the whirlpool of Corrievreckan. The flood tide rushes through the narrow sound at speeds of up to 8.5 knots before reaching the place where a great pyramidal rock rises from the seabed 719 feet (219m) below to a depth of only 95 feet (29m), forming the great whirlpool. There are few more awesome examples of raw natural power – the sound can be heard over 10 miles (16.1km) away.

A secluded bay on the floral island of Gigha

ISLAY WILDLIFE

The shores of Islay provide a wide variety of habitats, with great expanses of sand as in Loch Indaal, rugged wave-exposed rocky coasts in the west and shingle on the southern coast, with small outlying islands where both grey and common seals are to be seen basking in the sun. The island is particularly rich in flora, on the machair and moorland, in the peat bogs and woodlands. About 110 species of birds breed on Islay, including the rare native chough, a member of the crow family, with the same glossy black plumage but legs and curved beak of startling red. Islay is most famous as an over-wintering place for geese, with 25,000 barnacle geese and 4,000 Greenland white-fronted geese arriving each October and staying until the following April before returning north to their breeding grounds.

Kilmartin village, at the head of the valley, overlooks a remarkable prehistoric site

DALRIADA AND THE CORONATION STONE

From around AD 500 the Scottish kingdom of Dalriada had its capital in the hill fort at Dunadd. There are traces of buildings on the hillside and defensive terraces around the summit. Carved in the rock just outside is an inscription in Ogham script – evidence of Pictish use of the hilltop – as well as a basin and a footprint that may have been used at coronations. Some believe that Aidan was crowned first Christian king in Britain here in AD 574 by St Columba, and that the stone used became the Stone of Scone, once in Westminster Abbey but now in Edinburgh Castle.

KILMARTIN Argyll & Bute Map ref NR8398

The waters of Loch Awe once flowed southwards through the glacier-formed Kilmartin Glen, depositing sediment on the valley floor. The area was occupied from early prehistoric times, when hunters settled here to farm, and the concentration of monuments that they left behind makes this one of the richest archaeological areas in Scotland. At Achnabreck is the largest group of cup-and-ring marked rocks in Britain, but even more impressive remains are to be found further north.

The tall, flat-faced Ballymeanoch standing stones and a line of burial cairns stretch towards Kilmartin village. Ri Cruin is a crescent of boulders in a grove, and carvings of axeheads and, possibly, a boat's keel can be seen on the stones. The three Nether Largie cairns are higher – especially the most southerly, with its large chamber topped by huge stone slabs. Central to the site is Temple Wood Circle, begun around 3000 BC and modified several times up to 1200 BC. To get the best out of this complex and fascinating area head for the superb interpretative museum in Kilmartin village, where there is also a fine collection of 9th- to 16th-century grave slabs in the churchyard.

Carnasserie Castle, further up the valley, is a well-preserved fortified house from the 16th century, built for John Carswell, Bishop of the Isles.

KINTYRE Argyll & Bute

At the north end of Kintyre and 38 miles (61.2km) from Campbeltown, Tarbert has colour-washed houses and the remains of a 15th-century tower house on the site of a former royal castle. The Campbeltown road follows the wind-swept west fringe of Kintyre, with wide views over to Jura and Islay, then the hills give way to gentler country towards the handsome port of Campbeltown. By the waterfront is the late 15th-century Campbeltown Cross, and near by an unexpected delight – the 1913 art deco front of the 256-seat Picture House. Davaar Island, reached on foot at low tide, shelters the harbour, and in a cave on its south side is a painting of the crucifixion by Archibald MacKinnon, dating from 1887.

St Columba landed near Southend at the foot of the peninsula – a ruined chapel and two footprints carved in a nearby rock mark the spot. A winding road eastwards goes to the Mull of Kintyre, with its lighthouse – a stark, windswept place, only 12 miles (19.3km) from Ireland. A single-track, hairpin road with breathtaking views over Arran follows the western coast back to Campbeltown; alternatively retrace your route up the B842, diverting west to Machrihanish, where the golf course is on the bay's edge.

North of Campbeltown, the east coast route is slow and winding, with tree-lined glens and fertile valleys. Up the valley from the battlemented castle by the shore at Saddell are the remains of Saddell Abbey, with its impressive collection of carved gravestones. Carradale, further up the coast, is a small village beside a beautiful sandy bay, while at Skipness you can visit the castle and eat fresh seafood.

DRY LAND SAILORS

Were it not for the mile (1.6km) of land at Tarbert, Kintyre would be an island. Before the Crinan Canal was built, fishermen would sometimes carry ships on rollers across the isthmus to avoid the long sea journey around the Mull of Kintyre. King Robert Bruce, too, had his ships dragged across to make a surprise attack on Castle Sween. But the most famous traverse at Tarbert was made in 1198 by the Norwegian king, Magnus Barelegs. Promised by King Malcolm Canmore of Scotland that he could include in his kingdom any island he could navigate around, Magnus had his men haul his boat over the land, while he sat at the tiller, thus adding Kintyre to his possessions.

The high lantern tower of Tarbert's church would have acted as a navigational beacon for sailors around Kintyre

Near the ruined Kilchurn Castle, the waters of Loch Awe are shallow and reedy

MOUNTAIN POWER

Ben Cruachan holds a secret – Scotland's first big pump storage power station. The Visitor Centre explains how water from an artificial loch high up on the mountain is fed down through the rock to turbines within the mountain. Off-peak power is used to pump the water back up to the reservoir. The highlight of a visit is a ¾-mile (1.2km) ride down tunnels to the huge turbine hall, 300 feet (91.4m) long and 120 feet (36.6m) high. The plants along the way are real – tropical species, which are thriving happily in the artificial light, heat and humidity of the tunnels.

LOCH AWE   Argyll & Bute Map ref NN1227

Glacial action reversed the waters of Loch Awe to flow through the dramatic Pass of Brander instead of through Kilmartin Glen. The longest loch in Scotland – nearly 25 miles (40.2km), more than a mile (1.6km) longer than Loch Ness – it is very narrow, and the north end is dominated by the peak of Ben Cruachan. You can take a steamboat trip from Lochawe village which includes the impressive ruins of Kilchurn Castle, set on what was once an island. Ardanaiseig Gardens, 4 miles (6.4km) east of Kilchrenan, are full of glowing rhododendrons and specimen trees beside the western shore of the loch. It is worth following the minor road south through Inverliever Forest, which offers forest walks and spectacular high viewpoints over the loch. The eastern shore road gives views of the loch's small islands, some with ancient chapels and burial grounds.

LOCHGILPHEAD   Argyll & Bute Map ref NR8688

Lochgilphead was once the centre of herring fishing on Loch Gilp, with a wooden pier stretched across the bay, but the fish mysteriously vanished before World War I. Mills and dyeworks followed their example, and, besides tourism and Highbank Pottery, where you can see porcelain being made, the main employer is now Argyll and Bute Council, which has its headquarters at Kilmory Castle.

The castle gardens, open to the public, were partly laid out by Joseph Hooker, first director of Kew Gardens. They are full of rare rhododendrons, and so is Crarae Garden, on the Inveraray road, planted round a spectacular gorge. A little further on is Auchindrain Township, a former crofting settlement which now gives visitors an experience of Highland life. Its houses have period furnishings and the barns are equipped with old implements.

LOCH LOMOND

Part of Scotland's first National Park (Loch Lomond and the Trossachs National Park was formally established in 2002), Loch Lomond has two distinct characters – the narrow upper loch is hemmed in by mountains, and stretches up into the heart of the Highlands, while the broad, island-speckled southern end is bordered by fertile farmland. Here, within easy reach of Glasgow, are some of the loch's most popular attractions.

Balloch, with its modern castle, country park and opportunities for boat cruises, sits astride the only natural outlet from the loch, and is a busy centre. Up the west side, off the well-used A82, is Luss, a smart estate village, setting for the television series, *Take the High Road*. Lomond's east side is quieter, offering walking and outdoor pursuits. From Balmaha there are good views over some of the loch's 38 named islands – especially Inchcailloch, once the site of a nunnery, and now part of the Loch Lomond National Nature Reserve.

Much of the eastern shore is within the 50,000-acre Queen Elizabeth Forest Park. The road ends at Rowardennan, from where there is a stiff climb up the 3,192 feet (972.9m) of Ben Lomond. To visit beautiful Inversnaid, approach from Aberfoyle or by ferry from Inveruglas – unless you are energetic enough for the walk along the West Highland Way from Rowardennan.

THE WEST HIGHLAND WAY

It is on the shores of Loch Lomond that the 95-mile (152.9km) West Highland Way, Scotland's first long-distance footpath, makes the transition from easy lowland walking to the more rugged terrain of the Highlands. Starting from Milngavie (pronounced Mull-guy) on the outskirts of Glasgow, the route makes its way north to Fort William, often using ancient and historic routes – drove roads by which cattle dealers reached market (like the Devil's Staircase out of Glen Coe), military roads instituted by General Wade to aid in suppressing the clans, old coaching roads and even disused railway lines. Walk all the way if you wish – experts recommend going south to north, to build up stamina for the hills – or take a short walk along the route; there is no shortage of spectacular sections, and you may see red deer and, just possibly, golden eagles on the way.

Loch Lomond is a popular recreation centre within easy reach of Glasgow

SPANISH TREASURE

There is an old treasure map, now on display at Inveraray Castle, showing the location of the wreck of a Spanish galleon that sank in Tobermory Bay in 1588. After the defeat of the Armada, many Spaniards attempted to get home via the north of Scotland. One such vessel was given supplies by the people of Mull, but the Spanish refused to pay, and even locked up Donald Maclean, who had come to collect the payment. He managed to escape, and blew up the ship, which sank in the bay. Confusion reigns as to whether the ship was a troop carrier, the *San Juan de Sicilia*, or a treasure ship, the *Florida*. Treasure hunters are ever hopeful, and still dive here in search of a shower of golden ducats, yet so far only a few coins and cannon have been raised. Perhaps the crew simply didn't have the means to pay the islanders for their supplies after all.

Brightly painted shops and hotels face on to the sheltered waters of Tobermory Bay

MULL AND IONA   Argyll & Bute

Take the time to properly explore and discover Mull and you will find it full of interest and beauty. Craignure is the main arrival point, and from Old Pier Station the Mull and West Highland Narrow Gauge Railway runs the extremely scenic 1¼ miles (2km) to Torosay Castle. This line boasts a real rarity – a modern steam locomotive, built in Sheffield in 1993.

Torosay Castle is actually a Victorian mansion, set in 12 acres (4.9ha) of superb gardens. The house is full of character and is enthusiastically shared with visitors by its resident owner – you are positively encouraged to sit on chairs, peer into cupboards and browse through the family scrapbooks. Near by, on a craggy point with wonderful views along the Sound of Mull, is 13th-century Duart Castle, centre for the Clan Maclean.

Mountains give way to pastoral scenery on the way to the island's capital, Tobermory, with its houses painted in jolly colours around the bay. Tobermory's tourist attractions – the Mull Museum and the distillery – are diminutive, just like Mull Little Theatre at Dervaig, which is Britain's smallest professional theatre. With just 43 seats, it puts on a summer season with two or three actors. Calgary, further on, has an interesting sculpture trail and the best sandy beach on the island.

West of Ben More, Mull's highest mountain, is the Ardmeanach peninsula, the tip of which is only accessible by an arduous 5½-mile (8.8km) path. Its main sight is a startling fossilised tree, 50 feet (15.2m) high and possibly 50 million years old. Boat trips round Mull sometimes give passengers a view of it.

Mull's main road, mostly single-track, traverses the moorland from the east coast to Loch Scridain and on across the Ross of Mull to Fionnphort, for the Iona ferry. South of the road is walking country, with a coastline of basaltic stacks and sea arches – wild and lonely, but full of beauty and fascinating wildlife.

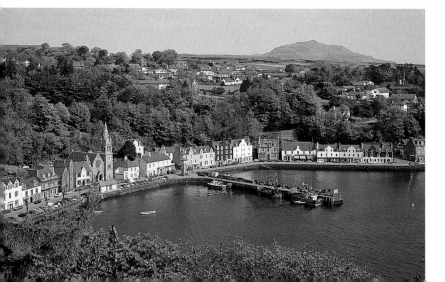

Iona is a magical place. Most visitors make straight for the abbey, but you should spare time for the remains of the 13th-century priory, built for Augustinian nuns. St Columba founded his monastery in AD 563 where the abbey now stands, and from it the light of Christianity radiated throughout Europe – the Book of Kells, now on show in Dublin's Trinity College Library, was illuminated here. Columba's foundation ended in AD 803 when Vikings slew 68 monks at Martyr's Bay. Later a church and buildings erected by 12th-century Benedictine monks were left in ruins after the Reformation, until restoration began in 1910. Now the home of the Iona Community, founded in 1938, the abbey welcomes pilgrims from around the world. Beside it is the ancient burial ground of the Scottish kings, among them Macbeth and Duncan. The abbey does get busy with visitors at times, but even though the island is small, it is possible to escape the crowds quickly and enjoy the fine sands and rocky landscape, the wild flowers and birds, and the view of the busy world beyond Iona.

Many visitors will approach Staffa humming Mendelssohn's 'Fingal's Cave' overture. He came to this extraordinary island in 1829, to visit the huge cavern on its south side. Here the volcanic basalt has cooled into its characteristic six-sided columns, making it look like a massive cathedral organ. Cathedral-like, too, is the enormous interior of Fingal's Cave; weather permitting, visitors are allowed to land from some of the many boat trips in the area.

The peaceful island of Iona has for centuries offered a religious retreat

DR JOHNSON ON IONA
Dr Samuel Johnson was not known for his love of things Scottish ('...the noblest prospect which a Scotchman ever sees, is the high road that leads him to England'), but even he was impressed by Iona. He arrived with Boswell on the evening of 19 October 1773 and spent the night, quite comfortably, in a barn. Next day they visited the priory – the nun's church was full of cow dung – and the abbey 'which is really grand enough when one thinks of its antiquity and the remoteness of the place', wrote Boswell. Johnson concurred. 'That man is little to be envied,' he said, 'whose piety would not grow warmer among the ruins of Iona.'

Dun Ara Fort, The Ise of Mull

This island walk includes two castles, a group of standing stones and the beautiful coastal scenery of northern Mull. It's an easy linear walk, with some scrambling on to one of the vertical circular outcrops which are such a feature of northern Mull.

Time: 2 hours. Distance: 3½ miles (5.6km).
Location: 3½ miles (5.6km) west of Tobermory.
Start: From Main Street in Tobermory, drive up to Argyll Terrace, following signs for the B882 to Dervaig. After half a mile (800m), where the B882 joins the B8013, turn right, signposted 'Glengorm 4 miles', and continue, passing the wireless station. In 1½ miles (2.5km), just before the cattle grid and bridge, pull into the left and park.
(OS grid ref: NM447567.)
OS Map: Pathfinder 302 (Tobermory)
1:25,000.
See Key to Walks on page 121.

ROUTE DIRECTIONS

Walk across the cattle grid and past the farm at Sorne, following the road right. After 200 yards (183m), take the left-hand fork up an unmetalled road, marked 'No Parking Here Please'. Continue up this forested road, past the rhododendrons and fuchsias on the right, until you see **Glengorm Castle**, with its walled vegetable garden and greenhouse.

Bear left and go through the gate at the two slatted barns, turning sharp right downhill through a short wooded section, passing through two more gates. The vista opens up and the road divides. Follow the path that leads straight on uphill. After 100 yards (91m) you will see three **standing stones** to the left below the path. Go down to explore.

Return to the path and continue to the brow of the hill. Cross a stile and walk along the left-hand side of a low-lying drystone wall, heading down towards the coast, crossing a fence by a ladder stile mid-way. At the foot of the field go through the gate, veer to the left around the foot of the bluff and follow the wide grassy track down to the coast.

The path snakes down to a long stone wall on the left, which turns at right angles near a river bend. Here there are loose boulders on the ground. Look towards the free-standing bluff nearest to the sea, pick out the faint grassy path and scramble up through a narrow gulley on to the flat top of the outcrop (take care in wet weather). Here the foundations of **Dun Ara Fort** can be seen, as well as spectacular views of the coastline, outbuildings of the fort and ancient terracing.

There are many coastal features around the seaward base of the fort to explore. Return to the start point of the walk by retracing your steps, with dramatic changes of scenery as you head back inland.

POINTS OF INTEREST

Glengorm Castle
The castle was built in 1860 for James Forsyth, the laird of the Dervaig Clearances, who asked a local woman for advice on what he should call his new home. 'Call the place Glengorm', she replied. Little did he realise that the meaning in Gaelic, 'Blue Glen', was a reference to the Clearances on Mull, when blue smoke raged from the burning homes of entire communities who had been thrown off their land. Glengorm was used as a base for sporting activities in the late 19th century and today is the most important location for the cultivation of vegetables on the island. It is privately owned.

Standing Stones
Mull has one stone circle, 14 settings and 13 single standing stones. The three standing stones, in a circle of boulders, that are to be found on this walk may not have been for sun or moon worship, as is so often assumed, but to establish a fixed calendar for agricultural activities – vital in ancient communities.

Dun Ara Fort
Dun Ara is one of four medieval forts on Mull, and the ruined walls are all that remain of its original three buildings. They are perched on the summit of a small plateau of Tertiary basalt lava close to Sorne Point,

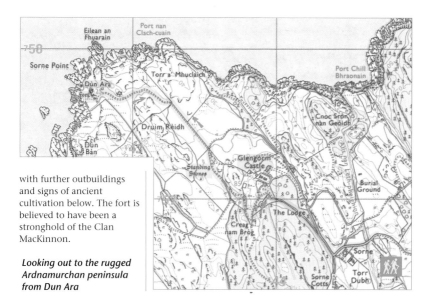

with further outbuildings and signs of ancient cultivation below. The fort is believed to have been a stronghold of the Clan MacKinnon.

Looking out to the rugged Ardnamurchan peninsula from Dun Ara

Around the Isle of Mull

A clockwise island drive of 75 miles (120km), which takes in interesting geological features, an important mausoleum and an unusual church tower. It is an ideal day trip from Oban on the Scottish mainland in the summer months, or you could choose to include an overnight stop at Tobermory, the island's main town.

ROUTE DIRECTIONS

See Key to Car Tours on page 120.
From the ferry terminal turn left on to the A849, which soon becomes a single-track road with passing places.
Torosay Castle and

Gardens and **Isle of Mull Weavers** are signed to the left; to visit them, take this turn, the weavers are near by, the castle is straight ahead. The formality of both the castle, designed by the Victorian architect David

Bryce, and the order of the terraced gardens, attributed to Sir Robert Lorimer, contrast strongly with this wild mountainous island. The 12-acre (4.8ha) gardens have an Italian statue walk, water garden, rockery and Japanese garden. In the nearby weaving workshop they use specially installed but noisy old dobby looms to make their own tweeds and tartans.

Return to the A849, turn left and continue to the signpost for Kilpatrick, where you can take a detour to Duart Castle (the name means Dark Headland), one of the oldest inhabited castles in Scotland. Home of the 28th Chief of Clan Maclean, the castle has a keep which dates from 1360.

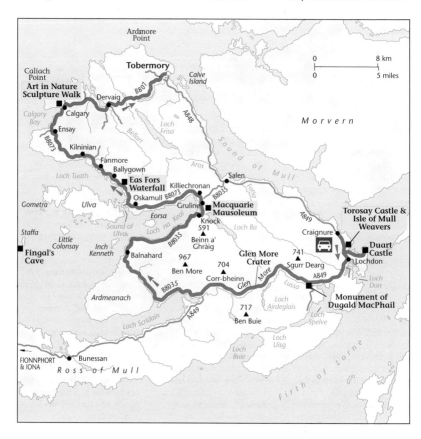

Continue on the A849 for vistas over Loch Don, a shallow sea loch with swans and other waterfowl. Pass the Old Mill Cottage Restaurant and continue towards Loch Spelve with its mussel farm, otters and bird-life. The road bears right inland, passing through mountains and the glen. At the junction signed 'Lochbuie and Croggan' is a squat stone cairn to the Gaelic bard Dughall an-t-Srth-Chaoil (Dugald MacPhail). Continue on the A849 driving through the forest on to open hillsides towards Glen More, with its waterslides and crescent of four small lochs in the valley below – the largest is Loch Airdeglais. Entering the broad treeless valley of Glen More you pass through the central crater of an extinct volcano, 6 miles (9.6km) in diameter. Descend to Loch Scridain, turn right at the junction on to the B8035 signed 'Gruline, Scenic route to Salen'. If you want to take a detour to Iona continue on the A849 to the jetty at Fionnphort.

Continue on the main drive on the B8035, passing Loch Scridain on the left. The road turns inland climbing up through the tree line to the top of the pass, with views across to Dutchman's Cap (Bac Mòr) and Staffa. The road then descends to Loch na Keal and Inch Kenneth and passes waterfalls above the road at Balnahard. Head along the narrow coastal road, with the island of Eorsa on the left, and continue over a hump-backed bridge. The road flattens out and passes over a series of small bridges. At the head of Loch na Keal the road passes through an avenue of rhododendrons by Knock Farm. Cross the River Ba and turn right to Gruline Home Farm to visit the **Macquarie Mausoleum**. Here lie the remains of Lachlan Macquarie (1761–1824), soldier, administrator and Governor of New South Wales. Known as the 'Father of Australia', he was noted for his reformist policies towards ex-convicts and for his record in public works. Macquarie was born on the nearby island of Ulva.

Return to the road and, shortly, turn left on the

The narrow road passes along the shore of Loch na Keal

B8073, signposted 'Ulva Ferry, Calgary, Dervaig', which rises up to wonderful views of the coastal islands including Ulva. The road passes Eorsa Island again and to the left is a magnificent view of Ben More, which, at 3,169 feet (966m), is the only Munro (mountain peak over 3,000 feet/914.4m) on Mull. Pass the Sound of Ulva and continue on to Loch Tuath and the spectacular **Eas Fors waterfall**. Continue until you reach Calgary Bay with its beautiful white sandy beach. Above the bay is an art galley and the **Art in Nature Sculpture Walk**. Carry on to Dervaig, built in 1799 by MacLean of Coll. Kilmore church has an unusual slim Irish-style round tower.

Stay on the B8073, which ascends passing numerous lochs, including Loch Frisa, to Tobermory. If you wish to take the ferry back to the mainland turn right on to the A848 and drive to Craignure.

You can't get far in Western Scotland without needing to catch a ferry, especially to its 130 or so inhabited islands. Many of the shorter routes are operated by local owners and provide an excellent service, but Caledonian MacBrayne – CalMac – is undoubtedly the name you will come across most. The company was formed in 1973 when MacBraynes, operators of shipping services, mostly to the Western Isles, since 1851, joined forces with the Clyde-based Caledonian Steam Packet Company, a youngster from 1889. CalMac sails to 23 islands and operates more than 30 ferries in a huge range of sizes, from the largest vessel on the Ullapool to Stornoway route to the tiny four-car ferry that plies between Tarbert at the top of Kintyre and Portavadie.

The view from MacCaig's Folly across Oban to the islands is spectacular

OBAN Argyll & Bute Map ref NM8629

To experience the true splendour of Oban, you should climb at dusk to MacCaig's improbable Gothic Coliseum and watch the glorious sunset over the Firth of Lorne and the mountains of Morvern and Mull. MacCaig, 'Art Critic, Philosophical Essayist and Banker' of Oban, engaged unemployed stonemasons on his spectacular tower from around 1897, and though it was never finished, it is Oban's most notable landmark. At its foot, the bay, sheltered by the island of Kerrera, is always busy with pleasure craft.

Much of the harbour front is dominated by hotels, and ferries for the Hebrides depart from Railway Quay. Here, too, is Caithness Glass where you can see the creation of jewel-like paperweights, and buy them, of course. Oban Distillery, in the heart of the town, welcomes visitors, and near by you'll find Geoffrey (Tailor) weaving tartans and making kilts for their shop.

Northwards, the fine tower of St Columba's Cathedral dominates the bay, and beyond it are the remains of Dunollie Castle, seat of the MacDougall Lords of Lorne. Further afield, Dunstaffnage Castle is worth visiting. This ruined stronghold, with gatehouse, two round towers and 10-foot (3-m) thick walls, stands on a rocky outcrop at the mouth of Loch Etive, and was once the prison of Flora Macdonald.

Across the Connel Bridge at Barcaldine is the Scottish Sealife and Marine Sanctuary, with its close-up – and hands on – displays of British marine life. To the south of the town is the Oban Rare Breeds Farm Park with a collection of rare breeds of farm animals, woodland walks and a pets' area. From here you can drive on to Arduaine Garden with its superb collection of rhododendrons and wonderful views.

Argyll and Kintyre

Leisure Information

Places of Interest

Shopping

The Performing Arts

Sports, Activities

and the Outdoors

Annual Events and Customs

Checklist

Leisure Information

TOURIST INFORMATION CENTRES

Ballachulish
(Seasonal). Tel: 01855 811296.
Bowmore
Islay. Tel: 01496 810254.
Campbeltown
Mackinnon House, The Pier.
Tel: 01586 552056.
Craignure
Tel: 01680 812377.
Dunoon
7 Alexandra Parade. Tel: 01369
703785.
Inveraray
Front Street. Tel: 01499 302063.
Kilchoan
Ardnamurchan (Seasonal).
Tel: 01972 510222.
Lochgilphead
(Seasonal). Tel: 01546 602344.
Oban
Argyll Square. Tel: 01631
563122.
Strontian
(Seasonal). Tel: 01967 402131.
Tarbert
Harbour Street (Seasonal).
Tel: 01880 820429.
Tobermory (Seasonal)
Mull. Tel: 01688 302182.

OTHER INFORMATION

Ferries
Caledonian MacBrayne Ferries.
Ferry Terminal, Gourock. Tel:
01475 650100. For Hebrides via
Firth of Clyde and west coast
ports; sailings to 23 islands.
'Rover' tickets available.
www.calmac.co.uk
Western Ferries (Clyde) Hunters
Quay, Dunoon. Tel: 01369
704452.
Forest Enterprise
Forestry Commision, 231
Corstorphine Road, Edinburgh.
Tel: 0131 334 0303.
www.forestry.gov.uk
Historic Scotland
Longmore House, Salisbury
Place, Edinburgh. Tel: 0131 668
8800. www.historic-scotland.net
Met Offfice
www.meto.gov.uk
Mull Tourist Information
www.holiday.mull.com
National Trust for Scotland
28 Charlotte Square, Edinburgh.
Tel: 0131 243 9300.
www.nts.org.uk
RSPB
Dunedin House, 25 Ravelston
Terrace, Edinburgh. Tel: 0131
311 6500. www.rspb.com
Scottish Tourist Board
23 Ravelston Terrace,
Edinburgh. Tel: 0131 332 2433.
www.visitscotland.com
Scottish Museums Council
www.scottishmuseums.org.uk
Scottish Wildlife Trust
Cramond House, Cramond

Glebe Road. Edinburgh. Tel:
0131 312 7765.
www.swt.org.uk
Weather
Mountaincall for West
Highlands. Tel: 09068 500441.
Born to Climb. Tel: 09015
600111. Weathercall for
northwest Scotland. Tel: 09068
232795.

ORDNANCE SURVEY MAPS

Landranger 1:50,000 sheets 47,
48, 49, 50, 55, 56, 60, 61, 62,
63, 68, 69. Outdoor Leisure
sheets 38, 39.

Places of Interest

There will be an admission
charge at the following places of
interest unless otherwise stated.
Achamore House Gardens
Gigha, via ferry from Tayinloan.
Tel: 01583 505254. Open
Apr–Sep, daily.
Arctic Penguin
The Pier, Inveraray. Tel: 01499
302213. Open all year, summer
daily; winter most days. Closed
25 Dec and 1 Jan.
Ardanaiseig Gardens
Four miles (6.4km) northeast of
Kilchrenan. Tel: 01866 833333.
Open end Mar–Oct, daily.
Arduaine Garden
On A816 20 miles (32.2km)
south of Oban. Tel: 01852

200366. Open all year, daily.

Auchindrain Township Open-Air Museum
On A83, 5½ miles (8.8km) southwest of Inveraray. Tel: 01499 500235. Open Apr–Sep, daily.

Balloch Castle Country Park
Balloch. Tel: 01389 722600. Open Apr–Oct, daily.

Boathouse Visitor Centre
Isle of Mull. (Ulva Ferry–by Aros) 8 miles (12.8km) west of Salen on the B8035 and B8073. Tel: 01688 500241. Open mid-Apr to mid-Oct, most days.

Bonawe Iron Furnace
Taynuilt. 12 miles (19.2km) east of Oban on A85. Tel: 01866 822432. Open Apr–Nov, most days.

Carnasserie Castle
Two miles (3.2km) north of Kilmartin, off A816. Open all reasonable times. Free.

Crarae Glen Garden
Minard. Contact Garden Department, NTS. Tel: 0131 243 9300.

Duart Castle
Isle of Mull. Tel: 01680 812309. Open May to mid-Oct daily. Grounds free.

Dunstaffnage Castle and Chapel
4 miles (6.4km) north of Oban, off A85. Tel: 0131 668 8800. Open Apr–Sep, daily; Oct–Mar most days.

Finlaggan Trust Visitor Centre
Islay. Tel: 01496 840644. Open certain days, Apr–Oct.

Inveraray Castle
Tel: 01499 302203. Open Apr–Oct most days.

Inveraray Jail
Church Square, Inveraray. Tel: 01499 302381. Open all year, daily except 25 Dec and 1 Jan.

Kilmartin Museum
Kilmartin. Tel: 01546 510 278. Open all year, except 25 Dec and 1 Jan.

Mull Museum
Main Street, Tobermory, Isle of Mull. Open Easter to mid-Oct, most days.

Oban Rare Breeds Farm Park
New Barran, Oban. Tel: 01631 770608. Open Mar–Oct.

Torosay Castle and Gardens
Mull. One mile (1.6km) south of Craignure. Tel: 01680 812421. Open Easter, then mid-Apr to mid-Oct daily. Gardens all year, daily.

Younger Botanic Garden
Benmore. Seven miles (11.2km) north of Dunoon on A815. Tel: 01369 706261. Open mid-Mar to Oct daily.

SPECIAL INTEREST FOR CHILDREN

The following places may be of interest to visitors with children. Unless otherwise stated there will be an admission charge.

Argyll Wildlife Park
Dalchenna, 2 miles (3.2km) southwest of Inveraray. Tel: 01499 302264. Open Easter–end Oct, daily.

Cowal Bird Garden
Lochan Wood, Dunoon. On A885. Tel: 01369 707999. Open Apr–Oct, daily.

Glenfinart Deer Farm
Barnacabber Farm, half a mile (0.8km) north of Ardentinny. Tel: 01369 810331. Open Easter–Oct; Nov–Easter by appointment.

Oban Rare Breeds Farm Park
New Barran, Oban. Tel: 01631 770608. Open late Mar–Oct.

Scottish Sealife & Marine Sanctuary
Barcaldine, on A828, 10 miles (16.1km) northeast of Oban off A828. Tel: 01631 720386. Open mid-Feb to Nov, daily; weekends only in winter.

Shopping

LOCAL SPECIALITIES

Distilleries
Bowmore Distillery, Bowmore. Tel: 01496 810671 (Visitor Centre). Open all year most days. Bunnahabhain Distillery, Port Askaig. Tel: 01496 840646. Open by appointment. Caol Ila Distillery, Port Askaig. Tel: 01496 840207 (by appointment only). Lagavulin Distillery, Port Ellen. Tel: 01496 302400 (by appointment only). Laphroaig Distillery, Port Ellen. Tel: 01496 302418 (by appointment only). Oban Distillery, Stafford Street,

Oban. Tel: 01631 572004 for opening times.

Food
Inverawe Smoke Houses, Bridge of Awe, near Taynuilt, 2 miles (3.2km) off A85 Oban to Glasgow road. Tel: 01866 822446. Open all year daily.

Glass
Caithness Glass, the Waterfront Centre, Heritage Wharf, Railway Pier, Oban. Tel: 01631 563386.

Pottery
Dunoon Ceramics, Hamilton Street, Dunoon. Tel: 01369 704360. The Highbank Collection Ltd, Lochgilphead. Tel: 01546 602044.

The Performing Arts

Highland Theatre
George Street, Oban. Tel: 01631 562444.

Mull Little Theatre
Dervaig, Isle of Mull. Tel: 01688 302828.

Sports, Activities and the Outdoors

ANGLING

There are ample opportunities for angling of all kinds in the area. Enquire at local Tourist Information Offices.

BEACHES

There are many sandy beaches all around this area. Calgary, Carradale and Kiloran Bay are particularly good

BOAT TRIPS

Loch Etive
Loch Etive Cruises. Trips on the loch from Taynuilt. Free transport from Taynuilt Station to the pier. Tel: 01866 822430.

COUNTRY PARKS, FORESTS AND NATURE RESERVES

Argyll Forest Park
Access from A83, B828, B839 and A815. Guided walks in summer. Tel: 01877 382383 Forest Enterprise, Aberfoyle.

Glen Nant Forest Nature Reserve
Two miles (3.2km) south of Taynuilt on B845. Contact

Forest Enterprise tel: 01631 566155.

CYCLING

Argyll Forest Park
Waymarked cycling routes. Tel: 01877 382383 Forest Enterprise, Aberfoyle.
Crinan Canal towpath (Ardrishaig to Crinan)
Contact Canal Office Pier Square, Ardrishaig. Tel: 01546 603210. Forest Enterprise Tel: 01631 566155.
Lauder Forest Walks
Glenbranter Estate, 3 miles (4.8km) south of Strachur on A815 (signposted).

CYCLE HIRE

Lochgilphead
Barmollock Farm, Kilmichael Glen, near Ford. Tel: 01546 810209.
Crinan Cycles, Canal Basin Yard, Ardrishaig. Tel: 01546 603511.

GOLF COURSES

Craignure (Mull)
Craignure Golf Club, 1 mile (1.6km) north of Craignure. Tel: 01680 300420.
Dalmally
Dalmally Golf Club, Old Saw Mill. Tel: 01838 200370.
Dunoon
Cowal Golf Club, off A815 at Kirn. Tel: 01369 702216.
Machrihanish
Machrihanish Golf Club. Tel: 01586 810213.
Oban
Glencruitten Golf Club, Glencruitten Road, 1 mile (1.6km) from town centre, follow signs for Rare Breeds Farm. Tel: 01631 562868.
Port Ellen (Islay)
Islay Golf Club, Machrie Hotel, 3 miles (4.8km) north of Port Ellen. Tel: 01496 302409.
Scalasaig (Colonsay)
Colonsay Golf Club, 2 miles (3.2km) west of Scalasaig Harbour.
Tel: 01951 200312.
Tarbert
Tarbert Golf Club, 1 mile (1.6km) south at head of West Loch Tarbert. Tel: 01546 606896.
Tighnabruaich
Kyles of Bute Golf Club. Tel:

01700 811603.
Tobermory (Mull)
Tobermory Golf Club, half a mile (0.8 km) north off A848. Tel: 01688 302338.

HORSE-RIDING

Dunoon
Velvet Path Riding and Trekking Centre, Innellan by Dunoon. Tel: 01369 830580.
Lochgilphead
Castle Riding Centre, Brenfield, Ardrishaig.
Tel: 01546 603274.
Oban
Melfort Riding Stables, Kilmelford by Oban. Tel: 01852 200322.
Port Ellen (Islay)
Ballivicar Farm, (trekking). Tel: 01496 302251.
Rockside Farm Riding Centre, Bruichladdich. Tel: 01496 850231.

LONG-DISTANCE FOOTPATHS AND TRAILS

Lauder Forest Walks
Glenbranter Estate, 3 miles (4.8km) south of Strachur on A815 (signposted).
Puck's Glen
A815, 5 miles (8km) west of Dunoon in Argyll Forest Park.
West Highland Way
A 95-mile (152.9km) walk from Milngavie to Fort William.

SAILING

Appin
Linnhe Marine Watersports Centre. Tel: 01631 730401.
Oban
Oban Sea School. Tel: 01631 562013.
Tighnabruaich
Tighnabruaich Sailing School. Tel: 01700 811717.

SEAPLANE TRIPS

Corrievreckan Whirlpool
Contact Tourist Information Offices for information.

WATERSPORTS

Appin
Linnhe Marine Watersports Centre (waterskiing, windsurfing). Tel: 01631 730401.

Glencoe
Glencoe Outdoor Centre (windsurfing). Tel: 01855 811350.
Oban
Puffin Dive Centre, Gallanach (sub aqua). Tel: 01631 566088.

Annual Events and Customs

Dunoon
Cowal Highland Gathering, late August.
Inveraray
Inveraray Traditional Highland Games, mid-July.
Machrihanish
Machrihanish Surf Rodeo, mid-August.
Oban
Kilmore and Kilbride Highland Games, mid-June.
Argyllshire Highland Gathering, late August.
Taynuilt
Taynuilt Highland Games, late July.
Tobermory (Mull)
Mull Music Fest, late April.
Highland Games, July.
Tour of Mull Car Rally, early to mid-October.

The checklists give details of just some of the facilities within the area covered by this guide. Further information can be obtained from Tourist Information Centres.

Inverness

Superlatives become quite commonplace in the Inverness district, which includes Britain's deepest area of fresh water, Loch Ness, and the highest mountain, Ben Nevis (4,406 feet/1,343m). In this area you will also find the most Arctic environment in Britain – on the plateau surrounding Ben Macdhui on the high tops of the Cairngorms. The Great Glen, a dramatic geological fault, slices Scotland in two, creating an exceptional landscape, and at its northeastern extremity is the town of Inverness, the 'Capital of the Highlands'. Here, too, are the mysteries of Loch Ness, the optimism of Glenfinnan, the bloody deeds of Glen Coe and the tragedy of Culloden.

LANGUAGE OF THE LAND
In Scotland lakes are lochs, and 'ben' means mountain. Like many Highland placenames, these are Gaelic words, and often give an idea of the kind of place they refer to – 'kin' (Gaelic *ceann*), for example, means head, so Kinloch means the top of a lake, while 'inver' (*inbhir*) denotes an outlet – Inverness is where the River Ness meets the sea. 'Tarbert' (or 'Tarbet') means isthmus or crossing place. Other pointers include 'ard', a height, 'ban' meaning white; 'beg', confusingly meaning little, and 'more', meaning great. It all adds another dimension to the landscape.

The red sandstone bulk of Glenborrodale Castle is superbly set above the bay

ARDNAMURCHAN AND MORVERN Highland
You can go no further west on mainland Britain than Ardnamurchan Point, with its spectacular views over to Mull, Coll and Tiree. The whole peninsula, with its rocky hills and desolate moorland, gale-blown trees and heather-capped promontories, has an 'end-of-the-world' feeling. The main road mostly hugs the northern shore of Loch Sunart, rich in birdlife, and you can take a minor road to Ardnamurchan's north coast as the main road passes round Beinn nan Losgann, or continue to the crofting village of Kilchoan, with its ferry to Tobermory. The 13th-century Mingary Castle, built on its sheer cliff to guard the entrance to Loch Sunart, is where James IV accepted the submission of the Lord of the Isles in 1495; Hanoverian troops built barracks inside it 350 years later. Make a detour to Sanna Bay for views to Muck, Rum and Canna and for superb wildflowers by the beach.

Morvern, across Loch Sunart, is a rugged land with gentler green glens. Lochaline, a popular yachting haven, is reached either by road along Glen Gleann, or by ferry from Mull. There are two castles in the area – the remains of Ardtornish, east of the village, and well-preserved Kinlochaline at the head of Loch Aline. The silica sands at Lochaline have been quarried commercially for manufacturing optical glass. Fiunary, along the Sound of Mull, was the birthplace of George Macleod, founder of the Iona Community. Caisteal nan Con is a small fortress guarding the Sound of Mull. The road ends 4 miles (6.4km) beyond, near Drimnin, with views towards Tobermory.

CANNICH Highland Map ref NH3331

The broad Strath Glass from the north leads to the modern village of Cannich where four valleys meet. Eastwards, down Glen Urquhart, is the prehistoric Corrimony Cairn, still with its stone roof and eleven standing stones. Glen Cannich is entered by a winding road between bare mountain tops, with groves of birch and alder. It widens towards Loch Mullardoch – its dam, at 2,385 feet (726.5m), is the longest in Scotland.

The approach to Glen Affric, perhaps the most beautiful of Scottish valleys, passes the popular Dog Falls. Along the 6 miles (9.7km) of Loch Beinn a'Mheadhoin are parking spots, many with fine walks from them. On the opposite side is one of the largest remnants of the ancient Caledonian Pine Forest, fenced to keep out deer and allow regeneration. Beyond the loch the road ends, but you can walk on to Loch Affric – a magical scene of clustered hills, birch and pine forest; in the autumn there is dazzling colour and the hint of snow on the peaks. You can follow the old track through the mountains to Sheil Bridge in Kintail.

Loch Beinn a'Mheadhoin lies in the lovely setting of Glen Affric

ATTAINING THE HEIGHTS
Until well into the 19th century everyone thought that Ben Macdhui in the Cairngorms, and not Ben Nevis, was Britain's highest mountain. It was the peak everyone climbed, including Gladstone and even Queen Victoria. She wrote in her journal, 'Nothing could be grander or wilder; the rocks are so grand and precipitous, and the snow on Ben Macdhui has such fine effect.' Like Everest, only recognised as the world's highest mountain in the 19th century, Ben Nevis remained unrecognised until accurate measurement was made by the Ordnance Survey in 1846 and the issue was resolved – Ben Nevis is the highest at 4,406 feet (1,343m), and Ben Macdhui is runner up at 4,296 feet (1,309m).

Lochan Mor and Loch an Eilein

A pleasant walk through the ancient Caledonian pinewoods of the Rothiemurchus Estate, passing three unique lochs and an island castle. It is a level walk, on well-marked paths, which can be shortened if required.

Time: 4 hours. Distance: 7½ miles (12.1km).
Location: At Inverdruie, 1 mile (1.6km) south of Aviemore on the B970.
Start: From Aviemore take the B970 south to Inverdruie and park opposite the Rothiemurchus Visitor Centre.
(OS grid ref: NH902109.)
OS Map: Outdoor Leisure 3
(The Cairngorms – Aviemore & Glen Avon) 1:25,000.
See Key to Walks on page 121.

ROUTE DIRECTIONS

From the car park opposite the Visitor Centre turn left and walk along the road for 100 yards (91m) to the junction. Turn left and in 50 yards (46m) go through the gate on the right signed 'Rothiemuchus Forest'. Head through the wood and over a stile on to open moorland. After crossing a second stile continue on into the forest, keeping right. Just before the brow of the third incline take a a small path on the right to view two lochans.

Return to the original path and continue to the ridge above **Lochan Mor**, on your left, renowned for its waterlilies. Turn right and continue to Milton Cottages. From the second cottage turn left, take the metalled road to the Loch an Eilein car park. At the far end of the car park take the path to the lime kiln, visitor centre and toilets, on your right. From the front of the lime kiln walk down to the shore of the loch and follow it around to the right, past the island with its ruined castle.

Continue to the pink granite memorial to Major General Walter Brook Rice, who drowned here while skating on thin ice on Boxing Day 1892. Leave the lake and ascend to the main path at Loch an Eilein Cottage. Turn left into the **Caledonian Pine Forest**. At the end of the loch follow the white footpath arrow pointing left. After 500 yards (457m) turn right on to the path which leads down to Loch Gamhna; for good views of the loch turn left after 50 yards (46m).

Return to the main path, continue and pass a cairn on the left. Turn sharp right over the footbridge for a second view of Loch Gamhna. Continue on the main path and keep ahead, ignoring the track to the right, and cross the little wooden bridge into pine forest. Continue straight on and follow the sign to Aviemore; do not take the Lairig Ghru drovers' road. Cross the footbridge over the stream and continue, passing through the wooden swing gate. Pass a cottage and follow the track around to the right, away from the loch, ignoring the footbridge down to the left. Go through the

Loch an Eilein Castle was a stronghold of the Anglo-Norman Comyn family

barrier and rejoin the metalled road by the car park. Fork immediately right uphill at the distinctive triangle of grass, on to a rising path. Go through two gates and pass a farmhouse and ruined buildings. Keep on and after 500 yards (457m) pass between two white buildings (the left one 'Blackpark'), and through an open gate. The road becomes metalled at this point. Carry on for 100 yards (91m) until you intersect the footpath which crosses the road. At the iron gate turn left on to the path signed 'Rothiemurchus footpath'. Continue and turn right to rejoin the original path from the Visitors' Centre and return to the car park.

POINTS OF INTEREST

Lochan Mor

This calm glacial lochan is particularly beautiful in the summer when its lily pads and flowers are at their best, and in the autumn when the birch trees change colour.

Loch an Eilein

Translated as the 'Loch of the Island' and famous for its ruined castle, there are also connections with the infamous Alexander Stewart (1343–1405) – 'The Wolf of Badenoch'. Grandson of Robert the Bruce, he earned his nickname by the razing of Forres and the burning of Elgin Cathedral.

Caledonian Pine Forest

The Great Caledonian Forest once covered all but the mountain tops of Scotland to a height of 2,500 feet (762m). Today the timberline is mostly found at 2,000 feet (610m). Pinewoods throughout Scotland have been destroyed since medieval times to make way for sheep, and when this became less profitable, deer stalking and grouse shooting took over. Rothiemurchus Forest is a rare survivor, giving some idea of what the native Scottish landscape once looked like.

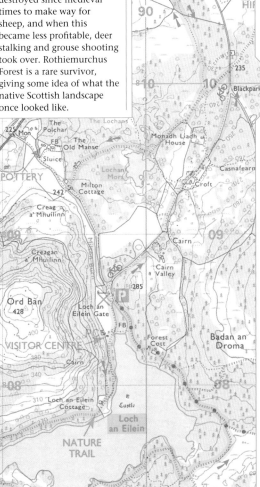

EARLY CAIRNS

If you think archaeological sites are dull, visit the fascinating Clava Cairns near Culloden, which opens a window on our remote ancestors. A site of major archaeological importance, and very beautifully set among beech trees, it has three large stone burial mounds, each surrounded by a circle of standing stones. They were probably built between about 2000 and 1500 BC. The two outer cairns, partly covered in small boulders, have stone-lined passages to the centre. The middle one is hollow, though with no passage. Instead, it has rough cobbled pavements leading away from it. Clava Cairns is part of a whole series of such monuments found only in the region of the Moray Firth.

A simple stone marks the spot where the Stewarts of Appin fell in battle at Culloden

CULLODEN   Highland Map ref NH7246

The Battle of Culloden marked the end of the Stuart ambition to regain the throne of Britain from the Hanoverians. On this bleak and desolate moorland east of Inverness, 5,000 Highlanders under the command of The Young Pretender – Bonnie Prince Charlie – faced 9,000 troops led by the Duke of Cumberland. It was 16th April 1746, a day of bitter cold, with snow flurries. The Highlanders, used to short skirmishes, were no match for the disciplined and well-armed soldiers, and despite courageous fighting were swiftly defeated. Cumberland ordered that no prisoners should be taken; all were killed, earning Cumberland his nickname of 'Butcher'.

Although it can be very crowded in summer, Culloden remains a moving place. The 1,200 Highlanders who died were buried in clan graves, marked by small, weathered stones. The 76 English dead lie in The Field of the English. Near by is the Well of the Dead, a spring where drinking Highlanders were killed. Coloured flags fly over the battlefield to mark the disposition of the armies, and the focal point of the area is a large 19th-century memorial cairn, built where the fighting was most ferocious. Old Leonach Cottage, thatched in heather, has been restored to its 18th-century condition; outside the cottage 30 of the Pretender's troops were burned alive.

The Visitor Centre, with an excellent slide presentation, has clear explanations of the battle, its causes and its aftermath. Prince Charles fled to the hills and eventually escaped to France, with Flora Macdonald's help. The clans were ruthlessly suppressed – the kilt, tartan, the Gaelic language and even the bagpipes were proscribed.

FORT WILLIAM Highland Map ref NN1074

Fort William's greatest asset is its close proximity to Ben Nevis, Britain's highest mountain, which stands sentinel over the Nevis range about 7 miles (11.3km) to the north. The town is also at the southern entrance to the Great Glen and at the head of Loch Linnhe, with routes to Badenoch and Skye, but this is not just a place to venture from – it has its own delights too. The idiosyncratic West Highland Museum, famous for its Jacobite collections, lives up to its description as 'an old-fashioned museum – it is full of information and surprises'. Treasures of the Earth, at Corpach to the west of town, is a huge collection of rare gemstones, crystals and fossils, including Europe's largest uncut emerald. Visitors can also discover gems of information, such as how amethyst crystals take a quarter of a million years to grow just one inch (5cm).

Until recently the tops of Scotland's mountain ranges were the exclusive preserve of the athletic, but now everyone can experience breathtaking views without so much as getting out of breath. Panoramic vistas to the upper slopes of Aonach Mor (4,000 feet/1,219.2m) open up from enclosed gondola cable cars which cover about 1½ miles (2.4km) in their climb to an altitude of 2,150 feet (655.3m). The ascent takes about 15 minutes and at the top, in addition to the views across Loch Lochy, the Great Glen, Loch Eil and the Inner Hebrides, you will find a restaurant, a sports shop, telescopes, interpretative plaques and slide presentations. There are a number of walks but do keep to the paths, both for your own safety and for conservation. Two recommended walks are to Sgurr Finnisg-aig (about 20 minutes each way) and to Meal Beag (about 30 minutes each way).

The faint lines of the Parallel Roads are a natural feature of Glen Roy

THE PARALLEL ROADS

In a quiet valley 18 miles (29km) northeast of Fort William is a geological phenomenon which is unique in Britain. Glen Roy and its side valleys are marked by three strange parallel lines known as the 'Parallel Roads', not roads at all, but the shorelines of an ancient glacial loch. Towards the end of the last Ice Age, 10,000 years ago, the valley was dammed with ice that melted in three stages, leaving these horizontal ridges along the valley slopes. Scottish Natural Heritage (formerly the Nature Conservancy Council) explains it all on an interpretative board above the car park. To get to Glen Roy from Fort William, go north on the A82, turn right on to the A86 at Spean Bridge, then left on an unclassified road at Roy Bridge.

The Water of Nevis

This well-established walk through the Glen Nevis Gorge, past superb waterfalls, takes in magnificent wider vistas, with a view of the summit of Ben Nevis and a ruined shepherd's cottage. A sturdy walk, with some steep and tricky passes, requiring reasonable agility and good footwear.

Time: 4 hours. Distance: 5 miles (8km).
Location: 5 miles (8km) southeast of Fort William.
Start: Take the A82 Inverness road from Fort William to the roundabout on the outskirts of town; take the second exit signposted 'Glen Nevis'. Drive up the Glen to the end and cross the river past the first car park, and on for a further 1½ miles (2.4km) and park in the car park at end of the road.
(OS grid ref: NN168691.)
OS Map: Outdoor Leisure 38 (Ben Nevis & Glen Coe) 1:25,000.
See Key to Walks on page 121.

ROUTE DIRECTIONS

Follow the path leading from the car park into the boulder-strewn and beautifully wooded Nevis Gorge, signposted 'Corrour/Rannoch', noting the Sheet Falls cascading down the side of **Ben Nevis** on the left. Continue into the gorge past fallen blocks of pink granite, and ascend through a wooded section stepping over any fords. The path may be slippery at this point, so take care when you need to ford streams or scramble over small rock outcrops, as the drop on the right is severe. The views of the falls on your right and those behind you are outstanding.

The fall of An Steall tumbles into the Water of Nevis amid the dramatic landscape of Glen Nevis

At the top of the falls you pass out of the wooded gorge on to a broad flat valley with an upland meadow backed by **An Steall Falls**. There is a distinct change in atmosphere as the rumble of the falls abates to be replaced by an eerie silence. Keep to the left-hand side of the valley floor. Follow the valley around the bend to the left. After 100 yards (91m) step across the river on to the sand bar, and follow the path to the other side of the bar in front of the reed beds.

Walk further into the valley along the side of the river, avoiding any overly muddy sections. Cross the wooden bridge over to the Steall ruins, once a shepherds' house, and carry on to the white quartzite path ahead which rises to give wonderful views back to the Ben Nevis massif (weather permitting), and the rugged Mamores on your right.

Stop after you reach the third side stream at the final rise before the path descends to the river. From here there are remarkable vistas in both directions. In the winter deer come down into this valley. Do not venture further, but return by the same route, this time taking in the view of An Steall Falls, and a look at the three-wire suspension bridge over the river before returning to the car park by the same path.

POINTS OF INTEREST

Ben Nevis
Ben Nevis is the highest mountain in the British Isles, at 4,406 feet (1,343m). The name 'Nevis' derives from the Gaelic *neimheas*, meaning 'venomous' or 'evil one'. The 'mountain with its head in the clouds' was formed around 350 million years ago through volcanic activity. The 5-mile (8km) track to the top typically takes five to seven hours to climb and descend, that is unless you are extremely athletic. There is an annual hill race here, the fastest time being a staggering 1 hour and 25 minutes. The tourist path up the mountain starts from the Visitor Centre by Achintee House. (OS Map Outdoor Leisure 38, grid ref: NN123729). Due to its altitude, the top of Ben Nevis is covered in snow during winter and spring, while its proximity to the sea ensures that cloud covers it for as much as 300 days of the year.

Glen Nevis
Described as one of the best glens in Scotland, and frequently compared with the Himalayas, Glen Nevis has been used as a location for many films, including, most recently, *Braveheart*. It is in fact a glacial valley carved out during the Great Ice Age, which started two million years ago.

Water of Nevis and An Steall Falls
Many falls rush with terrifying power like a curtain through this dramatic gorge. The Upper Falls of Nevis is, at 350 feet (107m), the third highest waterfall in Britain, after Glomach in Wester Ross and Eas Coul Aulin in Sutherland. An Steall Bhan in translation means 'the White Spout'.

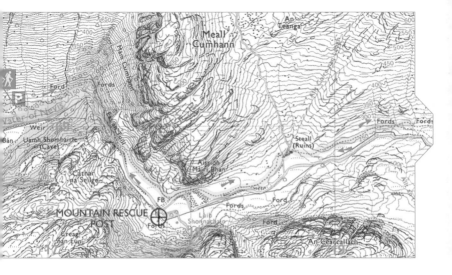

Glen Coe's skiing may not be as fashionable as Klosters', but it can be just as exciting. From White Corries at the top of the glen, where the fascinating Museum of Scottish Skiing and Mountaineering puts the sport into perspective, a chairlift takes skiers (and summer visitors, too) high into the mountains, with superb views to Rannoch Moor and beyond. There are 15 runs catering for all abilities, some with intriguing names – Fly Paper, for example, and Mug's Alley. Instruction is available, too. If hurtling downhill doesn't appeal, the Glen Coe area offers cross-country skiing, ski mountaineering, speed skating, snowboarding and even paragliding.

Looking down the steep valley of Glen Coe, with the Three Sisters peaks away to the left

GLEN COE AND RANNOCH MOOR Highland/
Perth and Kinross Map ref NN1058/NN3052

On 13 February 1692 the Campbells defied the traditions of Highland hospitality and massacred 38 members of the Macdonald clan in Glen Coe. Alastair Macdonald, like many clansmen reluctant to accept William and Mary as monarchs, failed to get papers attesting his loyalty to a magistrate by the deadline, the end of 1691, though they did arrive in Edinburgh in the new year. However, the papers were suppressed by the Under Secretary of State, who then told Campbell of Glenlyon that the Macdonalds 'must all be slaughtered'. Campbell and his men, pretending to be delayed on a journey, were accommodated by the Macdonalds in Glen Coe for a fortnight, then cold-bloodedly slaughtered their hosts.

The atrocity took place in the lower glen by Glencoe village, where the heather-roofed museum has displays of Highland life. The most dramatic part of Glen Coe is higher up. From the roof of the National Trust for Scotland visitor centre there is a fine view of outstanding mountain scenery of stark peaks and glittering waterfalls. You can find out about the many exhilarating walks from the visitor centre; there is challenging climbing, too, for the experienced.

Southeast of Glen Coe, Rannoch Moor is a vast expanse of peat bog, treacherous even in the driest season. Rannoch actually means 'watery' in Gaelic. The finest view is perhaps from the railway as it crosses on its way north to Fort William, but the best approach by car is along Loch Rannoch. On its south side is the Black Wood of Rannoch, native Caledonian forest of ancient

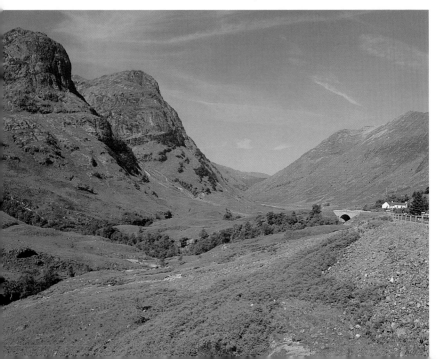

pines and groves of alder, birch and juniper. Just beyond Bridge of Gaur is a house built as barracks for Hanoverian troops after Culloden – a bleak posting. Rannoch Station is the end of the road, though it is possible to walk from here on old tracks. In places you will come across the blackened stumps of ancient trees protruding from the peat, as evidence that this forlorn place was once covered in forest.

GLENELG Highland Map ref NG8119

The old military road that leads to Glenelg rockets off the main Kyle of Lochalsh road, climbing rapidly up the Mam Ratagain pass to a viewpoint offering stunning views of the Five Sisters of Kintail above Loch Duich. There follows a gentler descent into Glen More, where a side road goes to the six-car turntable ferry that is a romantic alternative to the new bridge to Skye.

The Glenelg road passes the gaunt remains of Bernera Barracks, built in 1722 for Hanoverian troops. Continue for 2½ miles (4km) into Glen Beag for Glenelg's most famous sight – its two brochs. The circular walls of Dun Telve still stand to 33 feet (10m), and are 13 feet (3.9m) wide at the base. Dun Troddan is more ruined, but in both you can still see the remains of the internal galleries and stairways.

Admirers of Gavin Maxwell's *Ring of Bright Water* will want to go further along the coast to Sandaig, where the author lived and kept his famous otters in the 1950s. The house he called Camusfearna in his books stood near the shore of the beautiful bay, but burned down and was demolished, on his orders, after his death. His ashes lie under a boulder here, and there is a cairn with an inscription to Edal the otter.

Beyond Shiel Bridge the road to Glenelg climbs steeply, giving excellent views down Loch Duich towards Eilean Donan Castle

SCOTS BROCHS

Only Scotland has brochs, those distinct, cooling-tower-shaped structures, built in the Iron Age, from around 500 BC to AD 100. Some 500 sites have been identified, mostly near the sea and in areas where timber was scarce but stone was plentiful. No one knows what their function was, but they were probably defensive – the name is from Old Norse *borg*, meaning a fortress. The open interiors had galleries and parapets, and elaborate internal staircases, all carefully constructed. The best-preserved is on Mousa in Shetland, with its 40-foot (12.2m) walls.

The Glenfinnan Monument is a poignant Jacobite memorial

CONCRETE BOB'S VIADUCT

The West Highland Railway gives wonderful views down Loch Shiel from the Glenfinnan Viaduct, and the viaduct itself is impressive. It was built when the line from Glasgow, which had struggled across Rannoch Moor to Fort William by 1894, was extended to Mallaig in 1902. Curving over 1,000 feet (308m) over the River Finnan, its 21 concrete arches are up to 100 feet (30.5m) high. The viaduct was designed for Robert MacAlpine (later Sir Robert, founder of the famous civil engineering firm) whose nickname was Concrete Bob. It is said that buried within the Glenfinnan Viaduct are a horse and cart that fell headlong into the concrete before it set.

GLENFINNAN Highland Map ref NM9080

Glenfinnan will always have a special place in Scottish history, for it was here that the event which Churchill called 'one of the most audacious and irresponsible enterprises in British history' began – the 1745 Jacobite Rising. The monument tower of 1815, with its 1834 figure of a Highlander, may not be on the spot that Bonnie Prince Charlie unfurled his father's white and red silk banner, yet it is most romantically set at the head of Loch Shiel, overlooking the wooded Eilean Glean Fhianin and the mountains of Sunart and Moidart. Climb the tower for the best views.

The clan chiefs were dismayed that the Prince had brought only seven followers, not the French troops they had expected. They were persuaded to join him only by the example of Cameron of Lochiel, who brought 700 men to Glenfinnan for the Prince. So on 19 August 1745 the banner was set flying, the Old Pretender was proclaimed King James III & VIII, with the Prince as his Regent, and the army – still only 1,200 strong – began its campaign. Taking Edinburgh easily and defeating General Cope in the 15-minute battle at Prestonpans on 21 September, they set out for London. But with little English support and no hope of French help, they turned back at Derby in December and met their doom at Culloden the following April. The story is vividly told in the Visitor Centre nearby, which also traces the Prince's journeys through the Western Highlands and Islands after Culloden.

INVERNESS Highland Map ref NH6645

Inverness is the 'Capital of the Highlands' and a popular holiday centre, set on the banks of the River Ness at the eastern extremity of the Great Glen. Commanding the east–west corridor to Moray and Aberdeen as well as the main north–south route through Scotland, its location has given the town a strategic importance that has resulted in a chequered history. The town was probably well established by the time of St Columba's visit in AD 565. Certainly King Duncan (*c*1010–1040), of Shakespeare's *Macbeth*, had his castle in the town, and various clan chiefs and disaffected Jacobites have stormed through the town over the centuries.

Today Inverness is a busy administrative centre for the Highlands and Islands and presents a mostly 19th-century face. Even the dominating red sandstone walls of Inverness Castle were rebuilt during Victoria's reign as a Sheriff Court and jail, with a monument to Flora Macdonald on the castle esplanade. On the opposite side of the river loom the two massive towers of St Andrew's Episcopal Cathedral, which contains an interesting collection of Russian icons. The Inverness Museum and Art Gallery has fine examples of Highland artefacts and displays on the archaeology, social and natural history of the Highlands, together with various exhibitions, performances and talks.

From the museum you can see the location of Craig Phadrig, a vitrified fort on a wooded hill west of the River Ness, reached by a steep forest trail. (See page 80 for an explanation of vitrified forts.) In Huntly Street next to the river you can visit the largest kilt-making workshop in Scotland – The Scottish Kiltmaker.

A HIGHLAND WINERY

Few visitors to Scotland would expect to be able to buy locally produced wines, but that is exactly what you can do at Moniack Castle, 7 miles (11.3km) west of Inverness, near Kirkhill. But even the south-facing slopes of the Highland hills cannot support grape-vines, and it is traditional 'country wines' that you will find here – elderflower, silver birch, mead and the delicious sloe gin. This unique Highland enterprise is housed in the former fortress of the Lovat chiefs, where visitors can sample the produce in a wine bar and bistro.

A brilliant display below the castle walls at Inverness

The Ness Islands and the Caledonian Canal

Starting in the historic town of Inverness, this walk quickly takes you out into the rural setting of the midstream islands on the River Ness and along the Caledonian Canal. Easy underfoot, on recognised paths and pavements.

Time: 3 hours (includes exploring one sight of interest).
Distance: 4 miles (6.4km).
Location: Inverness.
Start: Park in the car park next to St Andrew's Cathedral.
(OS grid ref: NH664448.)
OS Map: Pathfinder 177 (Inverness & Culloden Muir)
1: 25,000.
See Key to Walks on page 121.

ROUTE DIRECTIONS

From the car park walk to the the River Ness, turn left and head downstream towards the bridge. Cross the river, towards **Inverness Castle**, to the **Town House** with its Mercat Cross. Turn right into Castle Street, passing the statue of Flora Macdonald, and take the right-hand fork down View Place and turn right to Ness Bank Church and the river. Turn left on the tree-lined bank to the old Iron Bridge and the memorial to the Great War.

From here you can see the River Ness and its islands. The river flows from Loch Ness, the largest volume of fresh water in the British Isles. After about 500 yards (457m) cross the footbridge over the river to the first island, walk over the next bridge, looking back to view **St Andrew's Cathedral** with its twin towers. Turn left along the wooded path with pine and beech trees, until you see another unusual curved bridge which crosses from one island to another. Listen to the small rapids, the thunder of water rushing around the islands, and the many waterfowl which are prevalent here. Keep to the

left-hand path as it encircles the island to the footbridge.

Cross the bridge to the west bank of the Ness. Turn left and follow the riverbank past 'The Generals Well' to the sign 'Whin Park'. (Dogs are not allowed in Whin Park, so dog owners should continue straight on here, to the end of the playing field.) Turn left, cross the wooden bridge and pass the miniature railway and picnic area. When the path turns to gravel veer to the left, pass the children's play area and walk around the lake, branching to the left at the end before turning right over the wooden bridge into a playing field. Keep left next to the river and continue.

At the end, near the weir, climb up a series of wooden steps to the **Caledonian Canal**. Turn right at the top

with the canal on your left, pass the rowing club and Jacobite Cruises departure point and continue to Bught Road. Turn right, looping back behind the stone wall and across the car parks, passing the Bught Floral Hall on the right and the Sports Centre on the left. At the Eagle sculpture on a traffic island turn right along the line of trees in the field and continue until you reach the River Ness. Turn left and walk downstream along the riverbank and make your way back to the car park.

POINTS OF INTEREST

Inverness Castle
Inverness was created a Royal Burgh in 1105 and, during the Scottish War of Independence in the 13th century, the castle was occupied three times by the English, until Robert the Bruce recaptured and

destroyed it in 1307. Mary, Queen of Scots, who was refused entry to a later castle in 1562, had the governor hanged from the ramparts. Today's mainly 19th-century sandstone building houses the Sheriffs Court.

The Town House
Built in 1878 in Gothic style, The Town House was once the business heart of the city where merchants plied their wares and public proclamations were made. Previously known as The Exchange, today it is home to the Council Offices. In 1921 this was the venue for the first cabinet meeting to be held outside London; the Prime Minister was David Lloyd George.

St Andrew's Cathedral
The rose-coloured, twin-towered Episcopal Gothic Cathedral was built between

Inverness Castle stands proudly above the river

1869–1874 to a design of Alexander Ross. Its many features include eleven bells, an octagonal chapterhouse, excellent woodwork in the choir rood screens and stalls, and stained glass by John Hardman of Birmingham. The most remarkable artefacts are five golden engraved icons, presented to Bishop Eden, the founder of the cathedral, by the Tsar of Russia in 1861.

Caledonian Canal
Along with the arrival of the railway, Telford's construction of the Caledonian Canal (1802–22) was responsible for the 19th-century development of Inverness. The canal links the lochs of the Great Glen – Loch Lochy, Loch Oich and Loch Ness.

CALEDONIAN PINE FOREST

The Rothiemurchus Estate has one of the few remaining naturally regenerating Caledonian pine forests, a precious survivor from the time when much of Scotland was clothed in native pines. Land clearance began in medieval times, when grazing was needed for sheep, and accelerated over the last two centuries or so until the very existence of natural forest areas was under serious threat. Fortunately this threat was recognised just in time, and what was left of the old Caledonian Forest has been actively preserved, offering a haven for the rare crested tit. No forest can be allowed to stand still, though, because survival also depends upon proper management. Rothiemurchus has been worked for centuries and its success can be traced at the Estate Visitor Centre. Guided walks can be booked here.

The Strathspey Steam Railway reopened for business in 1978

KINGUSSIE   Highland Map ref NH7500

The little town of Kingussie lies in the beautiful Spey Valley and is home to the Highland Folk Museum, a fascinating place with both indoor and outdoor exhibits. The main house contains traditional furniture and bygones, and a representation of a Highland kitchen; outside you will find a reconstructed Hebridean mill, a salmon smokehouse and a primitive black house from Lewis. There are regular craft demonstrations during the summer months.

Half a mile (0.8km) southeast of the town are the impressive Ruthven Barracks, built in 1718 to help subdue the Highlands. Despite being set on fire by the fleeing Jacobite army in 1746, there are considerable remains. The adjacent Insh Marshes Reserve (RSPB) has bird hides and nature trails. You can walk from here to beautiful Glen Tromie (see Walk on page 48).

To the southwest a little stream rises, flows east and then northwards picking up tributaries along the way. This is the famous River Spey, one of the foremost salmon rivers in Scotland. The broad Spey Valley is equally renowned for the quality of the malt whisky produced hereabouts – you'll not travel far without spotting the distinctive pointed chimney-caps of a distillery, for there are more than 30 along the river and its tributaries. Pick up the official Malt Whisky Trail for a tour of some of Scotland's finest.

Further north, at Aviemore, the dramatic mountain scenery can be viewed from the comfort of the Strathspey Steam Railway, which runs for 5 miles (8km) to Boat of Garten. Aviemore is also well known as a winter sports centre, its centre purpose-built in the 1960s to resemble a planner's dream of an alpine resort. The ski road links the town to the ski area on the edge of the

Cairngorm Plateau. A funicular railway now trundles up the slopes all year round, giving visitors a fine view of what will be Scotland's second National Park.

LOCH NESS   Highland

It would be difficult for anyone but the most hardened sceptic to gaze out over the waters of Loch Ness without just the small hope of seeing something which might be interpreted as a 'sighting'. Mentioned as long ago as the 7th century, when St Adamnan's *Life of St Columba* tells of the saint calming the creature down after an apparent attack on a monk, the Loch Ness Monster – or, familiarly, Nessie – has become the focus of the tourist industry here. There is a Loch Ness Lodge Visitor Centre with a large-screen cinema, exhibition and sonar scanning cruises; the Official Loch Ness Monster Exhibition in Drumnadrochit has audio-visuals and a 'life-size' model of Nessie; the Original Loch Ness Visitor Centre offers films and boat trips. You can hire a cabin cruiser, or visit ruined Urquhart Castle on the shores of the loch, from where most sightings have been made.

Monster or no, Loch Ness is beautiful and it contains more water than all the lakes and reservoirs in England and Wales put together. It is 24 miles (38.6km) long, one mile (1.6km) wide and 750 feet (228.6m) deep, making it one of the largest bodies of fresh water in Europe. The loch forms a major part of the Caledonian Canal, which links the west coast with the Moray Firth, and follows the line of the Great Glen, cutting Scotland in two. This spectacular geological fault has provided a way through the mountains for centuries of travellers and is followed today by the A82 between Fort William and Inverness.

Urquhart Castle is a popular place for Nessie-spotting

THE CALEDONIAN CANAL
One of the greatest feats of 19th-century engineering, the Caledonian Canal was constructed along the Great Glen by Thomas Telford, who took advantage of the lochs – Lochy, Oich and Ness – which account for about two-thirds of the route. The linking sections of canal have a total of 28 locks, including the famous 'Neptune's Staircase', a series of eight locks at Banavie outside Fort William. Opened in 1822, the canal was originally constructed to provide a safe route for maritime traffic, which had previously had to brave the hazardous seas around the north of Scotland, but the scenic route was soon appreciated by tourists too. By 1900 they were filling three steamboats a day, bound from Inverness to Fort Augustus, Fort William and Oban. Many cruise ships still operate on the canal.

Ruthven Barracks and Insh Marshes

A superb walk across heather-covered moors to a secluded wooded glen and the Insh Marshes Reserve. There are a few high stiles over deer fences, and binoculars are an advantage. The moorland is used by red deer in winter and there is occasional grouse shooting in September, but this should not create any access difficulties.

Time: 4 hours. Distance: 7 miles (11.3km).
Location: On the B970 half a mile (0.8km) south of Kingussie.
Start: In the car park opposite Ruthven Barracks.
(OS grid ref: NN764996.)
OS Map: Pathfinder 253 (Newtonmore)
1:25,000.
See Key to Walks on page 121.

ROUTE DIRECTIONS

After visiting the remains of **Ruthven Barracks** walk back to the end of the car park, up the bank to a small farm gate and on to a double farm track. Go through a second gate and up through the fields, looking out for views back down to Ruthven, Kingussie, the Spey and Insh Marshes. Keep with the path, looking down to the Burn of Ruthven on your left. On the grassy single track, turn left through the gap in the drystone wall, just before the ruined house. Cross the A-frame ladder over the deer fence, and head down to, and across, the burn.

Take the wide grassy path ahead sweeping uphill past distant television masts on Beinn Bhuidhe. Heather and grouse butts (dug-outs used by grouse-shooters) can be seen on your left. The path veers to the right uphill on to a heather-covered grouse moor. Keep to the well-marked pathway, noticing how the moorland is burnt in patches, to stimulate new growth of heather for the grouse. Near the top veer left leaving the main path for a narrow flat track leading up to a line of fence posts on the horizon. Pass through on to a beautiful broad heather moor with cairns. Eventually the path drops downhill past more cairns to a deer fence with a high stile.

Climb the ladder and head downhill into Glentromie with its mature birch woodland and the magnificent River Tromie. Many species of birds can be seen here. Descend into Glentromie and follow waymarkers and duckboards, keeping to the left, well away from Glen Tromie Lodge, and over the fence until you meet the path along the west bank of the River Tromie. This path eventually emerges beside Torcroy on the B970. From here turn left, and head back along the B970 to Ruthven Barracks, looking out for the RSPB signpost for the **Insh Marshes Reserve**, with its nature trails and bird hides.

POINTS OF INTEREST

Ruthven Barracks
On a mound overlooking the River Spey, these impressive remains date from 1718 and were built after the 1715 rebellion, ostensibly to restore law and order to the region. They replaced a 14th-century castle, and housed Hanoverian forces during the Jacobite rising, but in 1746 they fell to the Stuarts, who set them on fire before making their retreat. The roofless main blocks, parade ground, guard houses and stable are always open.

Red Grouse
Most grouse moors came into existence between 1800 and 1840, reaching their peak in the 1860s, with the introduction of the breach-loading gun. Until recently grouse moors covered three million acres of Scotland. Grouse are the most widespread game birds in the British Isles, and although population numbers fluctuate periodically, the recent declining numbers are currently causing concern. Their popularity as a game bird stems from their extremely fast flight when driven by beaters over carefully situated gun butts. The Highlands are their native stronghold, and populations increase with good moor management, through rotational patchwork burning, ensuring continuous new growth of ling heather shoots, their staple diet.

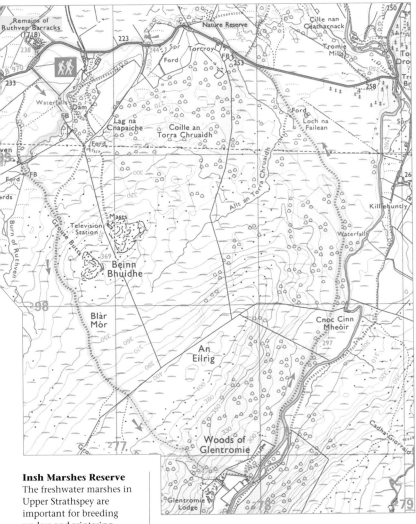

Insh Marshes Reserve

The freshwater marshes in Upper Strathspey are important for breeding waders and wintering waterfowl. Flocks of whooper swans from Iceland overwinter here between late September and April, and a variety of waterfowl, including mallard, teal, widgeon and tufted duck are resident in the winter months. There is also a population of roe deer who come to feed here.

The intimidating walls of Ruthven Barracks still stand

WEST HIGHLAND LINE
Mallaig is the terminus of the West Highland Line, which is celebrated as one of Britain's most scenic railway routes. Its construction was no easy task – the peat bogs of Rannoch Moor were traversed with a floating bed of brushwood, beneath tonnes of ash and earth; the rocky heights of Glenfinnan and the deeply indented coastline had to be crossed. Contractor Robert MacAlpine pioneered the structural use of concrete, building the high viaducts which give such magnificent views. Sit on the left for the outward journey (reserve a seat at peak times).

The lonely little church by the railway line to Mallaig has provided a location for several films

MALLAIG Highland Map ref NM6796

This small, busy fishing harbour, facing the Isle of Skye across the Sound of Sleat, stands at the end of the A830 from Fort William, more romantically known as the 'Road to the Isles'. The term comes from the cattle-droving days, before the railway arrived in 1901, but it holds the evocative promise of a special destination for today's travellers. It is also the last stop on the famous West Highland Line, and ferries from Mallaig can take you on to Skye, Rum, Eigg, Muck and Canna.

A couple of miles away at Morar the waters of Scotland's deepest freshwater loch tumble down a spectacular waterfall and into a beautiful sandy bay. One of the lovely beaches along here provided the setting for the film *Local Hero*, and the drive southwards is enchanting, passing through woodland of beech, oak and birch, with fine views out to the islands. Give yourself plenty of time here – it's a slow, winding road and largely single track until you reach the little church above Lochailort.

This part of the west coast has many associations with Prince Charles Edward Stuart. It was at Loch Nan Uamh, south of Arisaig, that the Prince landed in 1745 to raise an army, and it was from here that he left for France after defeat at Culloden the following year, leaving in his wake a tide of government retribution against the Highlanders.

Inverness

Leisure Information

Places of Interest

Shopping

The Performing Arts

Sports, Activities

and the Outdoors

Annual Events and Customs

Checklist ✔

Leisure Information

TOURIST INFORMATION CENTRES

Aviemore
Grampian Road. Tel: 01479 810363.
Daviot Wood
A9, by Inverness (Seasonal). Tel: 01463 772203.
Fort Augustus
Car park (Seasonal). Tel: 01320 366367.
Fort William
Cameron Square. Tel: 01397 70 3781.
Grantown-on-Spey
High Street (Seasonal) Tel: 01479 872773.
Inverness
Castle Wynd. Tel: 01463 234353.
Kingussie
Information stand in Highland Folk Museum.
Kyle of Lochalsh
Car park (seasonal). Tel: 01599 534276.
Mallaig, The Harbour
(Seasonal.)
Tel: 01687 462170.
Ralia
A9, south of Newtonmore; in car park (Seasonal). Tel: 01540 673253.
Spean Bridge
(Seasonal.)
Tel: 01397 712576.

OTHER INFORMATION

Ferries
Caledonian MacBrayne Ferries, Ferry Terminal, Gourock. Tel: 01475 650100. For Hebrides via Firth of Clyde and west-coast ports; sailings to 23 islands. 'Rover' tickets available. www.calmac.co.uk
Forest Enterprise
Forestry Commision, 231 Corstorphine Road, Edinburgh. Tel: 0131 334 0303. www.forestry.gov.uk
Historic Scotland
Longmore House, Salisbury Place, Edinburgh. Tel: 0131 668 8800. www.historic-scotland.net
National Trust for Scotland
28 Charlotte Square, Edinburgh. Tel: 0131 243 9300. www.nts.org.uk
RSPB
Dunedin House, 25 Ravelston Terrace, Edinburgh. Tel: 0131 311 6500. www.rspb.com
Scottish Tourist Board
23 Ravelston Terrace, Edinburgh. Tel: 0131 332 2433. www.visitscotland.com
Scottish Wildlife Trust
Cramond House, Cramond Glebe Road. Edinburgh. Tel: 0131 312 7765. www.swt.org.uk
Weather
Mountaincall for West Highlands, Tel: 09068 500441.
Born to Climb. Tel: 09015 600111.
Mountaincall for East Highlands Tel: 09068 500442. Weathercall for northwest Scotland. Tel: 09068 232795.

ORDNANCE SURVEY MAPS
Landranger 1:50,000 sheet numbers 25, 26, 33, 34, 35, 36, 40, 41, 42, 43, 49, 50, 51. Outdoor Leisure 1:25,000 sheet number 8.

Places of Interest:

There will be an admission charge at the following places of interest unless otherwise stated.
Ardnamurchan Point Visitor Centre
Tel: 01972 510210. Open Apr–Oct, daily.
Clan MacPherson House and Museum
Newtonmore. Tel: 01540 673332. Open Apr–Oct, most days. Donations welcome.
Clava Cairns
Off B9006, signed from B9091. 6 miles (9.6km) east of Inverness close to Culloden Battlefield. Tel: 0131 668 8800. Always open. Free.
Corrimony Cairn
Glen Urquhart. 8 miles (12.8km) west of Drumnadrochit. Tel: 0131 668 8800. Always open.

Culloden Battlefield
(NTS) Culloden Moor. B9006, 5 miles (8km) east of Inverness. Tel: 01463 790607. Open site all year daily; visitor centre mid-Jan to late Dec daily.

Eilean Donan Castle
Off the A87 at Dornie. Tel: 01599 555202. Open Easter–Oct, daily; limited opening Mar and Nov.

Glencoe and North Lorn Folk Museum
Glencoe village. Open weeks Easter and Whitsun–Sep, most days.

Glencoe Visitor Centre
Glencoe. Tel: 01855 811307. Open Mar–Oct.

Glenelg Brochs
Twelve miles (19.3km) west of Shiel Bridge. Tel: 0131 668 8800. Always open. Free.

Glenmore Natural History Centre
Ardnamurchan. Tel: 01972 500209. Open Apr–Oct, daily.

Highland Folk Museum
Kingussie. Tel: 01540 661307. Open all year, most days. Closed weekends Nov–Mar.

Inverness Museum and Art Gallery
Castle Wynd, Inverness. Tel: 01463 237114. Open all year, most days. Free.

Landmark Highland Heritage and Adventure Park
Carrbridge. Tel: 01479 841613. Open all year, daily, except 25 Dec.

Lochalsh Woodland Garden
(NTS). Off A87, 3 miles (4.8km) east of Kyle of Lochalsh. Tel: 01599 566207 or 0131 243 9300 (head office). Open all year, daily.

Loch an Eilein Visitor Centre
Rothiemurchus Estate, On B970 2½ miles (4km) south of Aviemore. Tel: 01479 811085. Open Easter–Oct, daily.

Mallaig Marine World
The Harbour, Mallaig. Tel: 01687 462292. Open all year, daily.

Official Loch Ness Monster Exhibition
Drumnadrochit. Tel: 01456 450573/450218. Open all year, daily, except 25 Dec.

Original Loch Ness Monster Exhibition Centre
Drumnadrochit. Tel: 01456 450342. Open all year, daily.

Ruthven Barracks
Kingussie. Tel: 0131 668 8800. Always open. Free.

The Scottish Kiltmaker
Huntly Street, Inverness. Tel: 01463 222781. Open all year, most days.

Strathspey Steam Railway
Aviemore–Boat of Garten. Tel: 01479 810725. Open Jun–Sep daily; certain days Apr, May, Oct, Dec and Jan.

Treasures of the Earth
Mallaig Road, Corpach. Tel: 01397 772283. Open Feb–Dec, daily.

Urquhart Castle
near Drumnadrochit. Tel: 01456 450551/0131 668 8800. Open all year, most days.

West Highland Museum
Cameron Square, Fort William. Tel: 01397 702169. Open all year, most days.

SPECIAL INTEREST FOR CHILDREN

The following places may be of interest to visitors with children. Unless otherwise stated there will be an admission charge.

Cairngorm Reindeer Centre
Glenmore, Aviemore (A951). Tel: 01479 861228. Open all year, daily.

Craig Highland Farm
Two miles (3.2km) east of Plockton on shore road to Stromeferry. Tel: 01599 544205.

Highland Wildlife Park
Kincraig. Tel: 01540 651270. Open all year, daily; weather permitting in winter.

The Performing Arts

Eden Court Theatre
Bishop's Road, Inverness. Tel: 01463 221718.

Shopping

LOCAL SPECIALITIES

Cloth
James Pringle Weavers of Inverness. Holm Woollen Mills, Dores Road, Inverness. Tel: 01463 223311 for details.

Country wines
Highland Wineries, Moniack Castle, Kirkhill. Tel: 01463 831283.

Distilleries
Ben Nevis Distillery, Fort William. Tel: 01397 700200. Open all year, most days. Dalwhinnie Distillery, off A9 on road to Perth. Tel: 01540 672219. Open all year, most days. Tomatin Distillery, 14 miles (22.5km) south of Inverness off the A9. Tel: 01808 511234. Open Mar–Oct, most days.

Pottery
Loch an Eilein Pottery, south of Aviemore on B970. Tel: 01479 810837.

Sports, Activities and the Outdoors

ANGLING

There are ample opportunities for angling of all kinds in the area. Enquire at local Tourist Information Offices.

BOAT TRIPS

Inverness, Loch Ness and Caledonian Canal
British Waterways, Inverness. Tel: 01463 233140. Caledonian Canal, Seaport Marina, Inverness. Tel: 01463 233140 (canal), or 01463 239745 (marina). Jacobite Cruises. Tel: 01463 233999. On A82, 1¼ miles (2km) from Inverness; courtesy bus from Tourist Information Centre. Loch Ness Yacht Charters, Dochgarroch, Inverness. Tel: 01463 861303. Caley Cruises, Canal Road, Inverness. Tel: 01463 236328.

CLAY-PIGEON SHOOTING

Rothiemurchus Estate Visitor Centre
One mile (1.6 km) from Aviemore. Tel: 01479 812345. Open all year daily.

COUNTRY PARKS, FORESTS AND NATURE RESERVES

Insh Marshes Reserve
(RSPB) Adjacent to Ruthven Barracks, Kingussie.

Glen Affric
South-west of Cannich off A831.
Contact Forest Enterprise,
Strathoich, Fort Augustus.
Loch Garten Nature Reserve
(RSPB) 8 miles (12.9km)
northeast of Aviemore off the
B970. Tel: 01479 831476. Open
Apr–Aug daily.
Reelig Glen
Moniack. A862, 8 miles
(12.9km) west of Inverness.

CYCLING
The Great Glen Cycle Route
Off the A82 Fort William–
Inverness road, through forests
on gravel surface. Contact Fort
Augustus Forest Enterprise
Tel: 01320 366322.

CYCLE HIRE
Arisaig
Bespoke Highland Cycle Tours,
The Bothy, Camusdarach. Tel:
01687 450272/0141 334 9017.
Fort William
Offbeat Bikes. Tel: 01397
704008.
Great Glen Cycle Route
Monster Activities, South
Laggan, Spean Bridge. Tel:
01809 501340.
Inverness
Highland Cycles, 16a Telford
Street. Tel: 01463 234789.
Spean Bridge
Nevis Cycles. Tel: 01397
712404.

DRY SKI SLOPE
Kincraig
Loch Insh Watersports and
Boathouse Restaurant, between
Kingussie and Aviemore.
Tel: 01540 651272.

GOLF COURSES
Boat of Garten
Boat of Garten Golf Club.
Tel: 01479 831282.
Carrbridge
Carrbridge Golf Club. Tel: 01479
841623.
Fort William
Fort William Golf Club.
Tel: 01397 704464.
Grantown-on-Spey
Grantown-on-Spey Golf Club.
Tel: 01479 872079.
Inverness
Inverness Golf Club, Culcabock.

Tel: 01463 239882.
Kingussie
Kingussie Golf Club, Gynack
Road. Tel: 01540 661600.
Newtonmore
Newtonmore Golf Club, Golf
Course Road. Tel: 01540
673328.

GUIDED WALKS
Five Sisters of Kintail
Visitor Centre at Morvich. Tel:
01599 511231 for information.
Rothiemurchus Estate
A mile (1.6km) from Aviemore.
Tel: 01479 812345.

HORSE-RIDING
Aviemore
Alvie Stables. Tel: 01540
651409/07831 495397.
Carrbridge
Carrbridge Trekking Centre,
Ellan Bridge Stables, Station
Road. Tel: 01479 841602.
Drumnadrochit
Highland Riding Centre. Borlum
Farm. Tel: 01456 450220.
Newtonmore
Croila Trekking Centre, Golf
Course Road. Tel: 01540
673742.

SAILING
Inverness
Highland Drascombe Sailing
School, North Kessock.
Tel: 01463 731493.
Loch Insh
Watersports, Kincraig.
Tel: 01540 651272.
Loch Morlich
Watersports, by Aviemore
Tel: 01479 861221.

SKIING
Glencoe Ski Centre
Tel: 01855 851226.
**Cairngorm Mountain
Experience**
Tel: 01479 861261.
Nevis Range
Torlundy. Off A82, signposted
'Aonach Mor'. Tel: 01397
705825.

SKI LIFTS
**Cairngorm Mountain
Experience**
Aviemore. Tel: 01479 861261.
Open all year daily, weather
permitting.

Glencoe Ski Centre
Off A82 by Kingshouse. Tel:
01855 851226. Open Jan–Apr
and Jul–Aug daily
Nevis Range
Off A82 north of Fort William.
Tel: 01397 705825. Open
Christmas–Nov.

WATERSPORTS
Abernethy Outdoor Centre,
Nethybridge. Tel: 01479
821279. Monster Activities,
South Laggan by Spean Bridge
(water skiing). Tel: 01809
501340. Loch Insh Watersports,
between Kingussie and
Aviemore. (Canoeing, sailing,
windsurfing.) Tel: 01540
651272. Loch Morlich
Watersports, by Aviemore. Tel:
01479 861221. Snowgoose
Mountain Centre, Corpach, Fort
William. (Kayaking, Canadian
canoeing.) Tel: 01397 772467

Annual Events and Customs

Aviemore
Sled-dog rally, late January.
Rothiemurchus International
Highland Games, late July.
Drumnadrochit
Glenurquhart Highland
Gathering and Games, late
August.
Grantown-on-Spey
Torchlight Procession, late
December.
Inverness
Folk Festival, Easter weekend.
Inverness Highland Games,
late July.
Inverness Tattoo, late July.
Kingussie
Badenoch & Strathspey Music
Festival, late March. Contact Mrs
Graham Tel: 01540 661349.
Shinty (Camanachd Cup Final),
First Saturday in June.

The checklists give details of just
some of the facilities within the
area covered by this guide.
Further information can be
obtained from Tourist
Information Centres.

The Hebrides
INNER HEBRIDES

This group of islands which lies off the ragged west coast of Scotland is steeped in the history and legends of the land. Skye is the largest and most northerly of the group – and the most accessible since the opening of the road bridge from Kyle of Lochalsh. It is also very picturesque, with the beautiful Cuillins rising up in the south before dropping to a coastline of deep indentations and rocky headlands. But each of the islands has its own distinctive charm: Coll and Tiree are low-lying and fertile; Rum is a National Nature Reserve; Eigg has its 'singing sands' and much geological interest; Muck is far more pleasant than its name might suggest.

BURROWING BIRDS

The elusive Manx shearwater, *Puffinus puffinus*, which comes in to land only under cover of darkness, has been breeding in burrows on Rum for centuries. The Vikings, alarmed at hearing their strange calls from underground, named the westernmost mountain Trollival, or 'the place of the trolls'.

COLL AND TIREE

Like Harris and Lewis, the low island of Coll is made up of Lewisian gneiss, the oldest rock in Europe, exposures of which can be seen in the rocky approach to the harbour at Arinagour. Inland, peat bogs dotted with lochans give way in the west to silvery beaches, with sand dunes reaching to a height of over 100 feet (30.5m). The crofting community here was once 2,000 strong, and rich pastureland led to production of the island's own special cheese. Today, visitors come to enjoy the peace and tranquillity, or to fish for brown trout in the lochans. There are many reminders of more ancient inhabitants, with the standing stones at Totronald, a cairn at Arinagour and a number of Iron-Age forts to explore – have a look at Dun an Achaidh and Feall Bay. In the south of the island, Breachacha Castle dates from around 1450 and was built by the

Breachacha Castle looms on the shoreline to the south of Coll

Macleans, one-time lairds of Coll.

Tiree's Gaelic name meant 'land of corn', and it is certainly very fertile. The island is low-lying and somewhat windswept, but this does not detract from its appeal to visitors – indeed, it is a positive attraction to those who come for the windsurfing, and is more than made up for by a record rate of sunshine. There are prehistoric remains to explore, including the broch of Dun Mor Vaul, and between Vaul and Balephetrish lies the 'ringing stone' which is covered with over 50 Bronze-Age cup marks.

These two neighbouring islands, northwest of Mull, can be reached by ferry from Oban, and Tiree has connecting flights from Glasgow.

RUM, EIGG, MUCK AND CANNA

Rum's four high pinnacles make it the most easily recognised of the Small Isles – the tallest peak, Askival, reaches 2,592 feet (810m) – and there are semi-precious stones in the rocks of these mountains. The only settlement is at the head of Loch Scresort, where the wonderfully eccentric Victorian Kinloch House, which you can visit, is a reminder of the days when the island was a private sportsman's paradise overrun with specially introduced red deer. It is a strangely desolate island, its crofters cleared long ago. In 1957 the Nature Conservancy Council (now Scottish Natural Heritage) purchased Rum. Today the island is managed as a national nature reserve and biosphere reserve, and gradually the native vegetation and wildlife, including white-tailed sea eagles, are being restored. Two nature

The circular walls of Tiree's Dun Mor Vaul can still be clearly identified

SAILOR BEWARE!
Scores of sailing boats take to the waters around the west coast of Scotland, which are a delightful, if challenging, playground. The Western Isles offer several distinctive hazards to sailors, quite apart from the expected rigours of weather and submerged rocks. If you are relying on your compass to find your way past Canna, then watch out, because Compass Hill, just to the north of the harbour, is particularly rich in iron deposits and is said to interfere with navigational compasses. And if you thought of taking a short cut between the islands of Jura and Scarba, think again – the Corrievreckan whirlpool could break you up in no time.

EIGG – A COMMUNITY-OWNED ISLAND

In 1996 the German owner of Eigg, an artist, put the island on the market. The islanders at once launched a public appeal, in conjunction with the Highland Council and the Scottish Wildlife Trust, to raise money to buy Eigg in the name of the newly-formed Eigg Heritage Trust. It was hoped that the trust would give the inhabitants both security of tenure and and a chance to direct their economic future. Donations of £1.5 million enabled their dream to come true and Eigg became the first community-owned island in Britain in June 1997.

The view from Arisaig's sandy shoreline to the steep peaks of Rum, with the cliffs of Eigg to the left

trails can be followed through the woodland from Kinloch House.

Washed in ever-changing light, Eigg has been likened to an upturned boat, its prow formed by the sweeping cliffs of the Sgurr (1289ft/393m), a dramatic pitchstone ridge to the south of the island. The sheltering rock wall has created a sub-tropical micro-climate on the island. The island flora, which includes rare ferns and palm trees, is incredibly rich. In the bay of Laig, to the north west, there are 'singing sands' of quartzite. Three hundred and ninety five islanders were massacred by marauding MacLeods from Skye as they hid in the cave of Uamh Fhraing on the southern coastline, back in 1577. The story is told in Sir Walter Scott's poem 'The Lord of the Isles'. Eigg was a base for the MacDonalds of Clanranald, but when the family fell on hard times in 1828 the island was sold, and a succession of owners have attempted to stabilise the crofting community here.

Muck, a mere 2 miles (3.2km) by one mile (1.6km), is the smallest, lowest and most isolated of the Small Isles. Gently sloping and comparatively fertile, Muck supports a small community which is successfully run as a model island unit by its paternalistic laird, from Gallanach House.

Canna is the most westerly and perhaps the most attractive of this island group, its northern cliffs noisy with seabirds. Spring arrives early here, and the land is comparatively rich and fertile. There are remains of an early nunnery on the island. Like Eigg, Canna was sold by the MacDonalds of Clanranald in the early years of the 19th century, and later attracted a succession of benevolent owners. The last of these, the Gaelic scholar John Lorne Campbell, presented it to the National Trust for Scotland in 1981.

SKYE AND RAASAY

Skye is the largest and most famous of the Inner Hebrides, dominated from every view by the high peaks of the Cuillins. The jagged gabbro of the Black Cuillins and the pink, scree-covered granite of the Red Cuillins have proved an irresistable challenge for mountaineers, and the most inaccessible peaks were only conquered at the end of the last century. To the north on the Trotternish peninsula is an extraordinary broken ridge from which peaks and pillars loom eerily on a misty day.

Road signs in Gaelic as well as English quickly tell you you're in a different culture, and Skye retains a strong Gaelic identity, encouraged at the college, Sabhal Mor Ostaig, in Sleat. At the Aros Heritage Centre, just south of Portree, a forest walk illustrates the letters of the Gaelic alphabet. The centre also offers one of the best introductions to the history of Skye. Through a 45-minute audio tour the story is told of the crofters and their struggles to survive the hardships of the land, famine and poverty after the 1745 rebellion. There are many tales, including one of a chieftain who tried to sell his people into slavery in the Colonies, and of the famous riots on neighbouring Raasay, in 1882. This civil disturbance led directly to the Crofters' Act of 1886, controlling rent and tenure for the first time, which is still in place today. Further crofting museums at Colbost and Luib have reconstructed homesteads.

The Uig ferry will transport you onwards from Skye to North Uist or Lewis

OLD MACDONALD
Duntulm was a Macdonald stronghold famous for its hospitality. However, the story is told of one chief who discovered that his heir planned his murder when an invitation to dinner was mixed up accidentally with the instructions to the hired assassin. The treacherous heir was thrown into the dungeon at Duntulm, with nothing to eat but salt beef, and no water to quench his thirst. The legend continues that in later years a skeleton was discovered still clutching an empty mug.

A FAIRY TOKEN
A threadbare scrap of cloth, faded almost beyond recognition and displayed safely behind glass, is one of Scotland's best-loved talismans. This is the Fairy Flag of the MacLeods, supposedly presented to a clan chief, back in the mists of time, by his fairy lover, who promised that aid would be forthcoming if the cloth were waved in times of dire need. The flag has been used twice to turn the course of battle, apparently with great success, giving the lie to spoil-sports who claim it is a banner stolen from Harold Hardrada in 1066.

Portree is the island's capital, its colour-washed houses round the harbour pleasing on the eye. This little town was named after a royal visit in 1540 by James V – *port righ* means king's harbour – and its formal square is a miniature delight. Portree is the gateway to the Trotternish peninsula; taking the road up the eastern side, look out for the distinctive column of the Old Man of Storr and other strange rock formations up on your left, and for the columnar formations and dramatic waterfall at the Kilt Rock on the coast to your right, just before Staffin – there are marvellous views from here across to the blue hills of the mainland.

Continuing around this long finger of land you pass ruined Duntulm Castle and a memorial to Flora Macdonald, the Jacobite heroine who smuggled Prince Charles Edward Stuart here from his hiding place in South Uist in 1746. The Prince, disguised as 'Betty Burke', continued his escape to Raasay and then on to France. Flora was arrested and briefly imprisoned in the Tower of London. She later married a Skye man and emigrated to America; they returned to live down the coast at Kingsborough, and Flora's grave is there.

Heading west from Portree brings you to the wilder side of the island, with the Waternish and Duinish peninsulas like two long fingers reaching out towards the Outer Hebrides. Dunvegan is the family seat of another powerful Skye clan, the MacLeods, and claims to be Scotland's oldest inhabited castle, occupied since the 13th century. Surrounded by a stout wall, and heavily restored and harled in the mid-19th century, the castle is impressive if not beautiful, but the treasures in its richly furnished rooms are well worth a look.

Heavily restored in Victorian times, Dunvegan Castle is the seat of the MacLeods of Skye

Looking across to Blaven from Torrin, on the winding road to Elgol

Broadford is the main centre for exploring the south of the island, and with its concentration of craftspeople, it is a good place to seek out good-quality souvenirs. Definitely not a place to get something to take home, but a good place to visit, is the award-winning Reptile Centre, or Serpentarium. Here you can handle snakes and learn a lot more about their way of life.

If the weather is clear, don't miss a drive over to Elgol to experience some of Britain's most magnificent scenery. The road winds below the mighty Red Cuillins and beside Loch Slapin before descending an alarmingly steep road into Elgol (not for caravans). You can see across to the island of Soay, with Canna, Rum and Eigg to the south. Try to make time for a boat trip, which offers a dramatic glimpse of spectacular Loch Coruisk.

After the barrenness of the mountains, Sleat seems a veritable Garden of Eden. Surrounded by the lovely Armadale Castle Gardens, the Museum of the Isles is well worth a visit. There are excellent exhibitions, genealogical research facilities, guided walks, a restaurant and much more. Look out for the special events which are held during the summer.

Skye is an unlikely crossroads among the islands. You can reach it by ferry from Mallaig (about 40 minutes), or across the strong currents by Glenelg (summer only), or across the new bridge at Kyle of Lochalsh. The bridge has provoked controversy, particularly over its tolls, but at least it is low enough to be unobtrusive and must be a relief to those who have watched the hours of their holiday tick away as they wait for the little ferry. Ferries to the outer islands leave from the harbour at Uig, on the Trotternish peninsula, and to Raasay from Sconser.

OTTERS

Many people hope to spot wild otters around the shores and lochs of Scotland, and, given a bit of luck, a good pair of binoculars and some local guidance, there is every chance you will. The Kylerhea Otter Sanctuary on Skye is a good place to learn more about these shy creatures, and to seek advice on where and when to look. Loch Sunart on the southern coast of the Ardnamurchan peninsula, Loch Spelve in Mull and Loch Eynort in South Uist are good places where you may see them.

Camasunary Bay and the Black Cuillins

Some of the most spectacular scenery on Skye, with magnificent views of Camasunary Bay, the island of Rum, and the Black Cuillins. A strenuous walk, which may be shortened by omitting the stretch to Loch na Crèitheach. Good waterproof footwear is recommended.

Time: 5 hours. Distance: 8½ miles
(13.7km), can be shortened to 6 miles (9.7km).
Location: 15 miles (24km) west of Broadford.
Start: From Broadford take the B8083 (formerly the A881)
signposted 'Elgol'. The road passes through Torrin and along
the shore of Loch Slapin. Drive past the sign for Old Kilmarie
Graveyard, and park in the layby on the left
opposite a farm gate. (OS grid ref: NG545172.)
OS Map: Outdoor Leisure 8 (The Cuillin & Torridon Hills)
1:25,000.
See Key to Walks on page 121.

ROUTE DIRECTIONS

Cross the road to the farm gate, ignoring the sign 'No footbridge at Camasunary', which is irrelevant to this walk. Go through the gate and walk uphill, over a burn, and towards the distant trees. As the path levels look down to the right where you will see a small lochan and the nearby remains of a stone circle.

Cross the stepping stones of several burns and follow the path up the steep slope towards Am Màm, passing through a farm gate. Here there are cairns and, over the top of Am Màm on the left, panoramic views of Loch Scavaig and the islands of Soay, **Rum** and Canna. Soon the magnificent sweep of **Camasunary Bay** backed by lush green meadows and the dramatic **Black Cuillin Hills** come into view. Loch na Crèitheach and the whole

route can also be seen from here. The path curves to the right and drops downhill. On reaching the hairpin bend turn right, slightly downhill. Alternatively, to shorten the walk, take the hairpin path to the bay and back again.

For Loch na Crèitheach continue on the path (boggy in wet weather), following the contours. Cross the pretty Abhainn nan Leac with its waterfalls, and head for the cleft in the rocks between An t-Sròn and Bla Bheinn. Walk alongside the stream and through the gap until the superb view of Loch na Crèitheach comes into sight. Descend the heathery slope on the path which now runs almost parallel to the loch; two-thirds of the way down you will see a drystone wall and the return path along the lochside. At an appropriate point walk down to the loch

through one of the dry gullies, turn left and walk alongside the loch. Head towards the beach of Camasunary Bay along the clear path ignoring the right turn which would take you around the foot of the loch.

Pass a ruined building and turn right behind the white house to walk across the meadow to the picturesque white bothy. Return to the house and turn right following the path over the wooden bridge. After the hairpin bend turn right and follow the path uphill to Am Màm and down to Kilmarie.

POINTS OF INTEREST

Rum
One of the most spectacular of the Inner Hebrides, Rum contains the earliest settlements of Mesolithic man to be found in

Camasunary Bay
One of the most beautiful bays in Skye, its Gaelic meaning is 'Bay of the Fair Shieling' (pasture). At the far end of the beach lies a bothy – once a dwelling for farm servants, but now a temporary shelter for walkers and climbers.

The Black Cuillins
This is the finest mountain skyline in Scotland, the Black Cuillins include some 20 peaks including 12 munros (peaks over 3,000 feet/914.4m). The name is popularly believed to be derived from Cu Chulainn, a legendary hunter who crossed from Ireland to

Peaceful Camasunary Bay opens out below walkers on the ridge of Am Mam

Skye in two mighty strides. A favourite haunt of climbers, geologists and walkers, the Cuillins have also captured the imagination of artists and poets, including J M W Turner and Sir Walter Scott.

Camasunary Track
The track to Camasunary was engineered by the army in 1968. It replaced a rough path and gave game fishermen better access to Loch Coruisk, around the next headland.

Scotland. The name of the island was changed back from Rhum to the Gaelic spelling Rum in 1991. The island is owned by Scottish Natural Heritage who are encouraging its natural vegetation and wildlife.

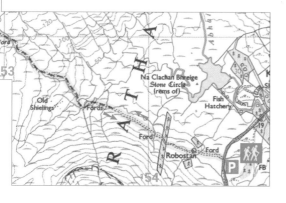

FLORA AND FAUNA

The coastline, freshwater, hills, moors and mountains of the Outer Hebrides provide a wide variety of habitats for over 700 species of flowering plants and ferns. Acid-tolerant plants, such as heathers, grow in peat, while the delicate wild pansy, silverweed and orchids abound on the machair. On the moorland lochs waterlilies are found, while at higher altitudes the alpine lady's mantle thrives.

This is also a birdwatcher's paradise, with more than 300 species recorded, at least 107 of which breed here. Cormorants, greylag geese, shelduck, common eider and whooper swans are often seen, and the elusive corncrake is still to be heard from the long grass. Red- and black-throated divers occur on the more remote moorland lochs. There are occasional sightings of the golden eagle and, on Benbecula, the short-eared owl. In the old woodlands near Lews Castle treecreepers and grey wagtails can be seen.

Castlebay, Barra with Kisimul Castle in the centre

THE OUTER HEBRIDES

Known also as the Western Isles, this chain of islands, which includes Lewis and Harris, North and South Uist, Benbecula and Barra, is linked by a series of causeways and ferry crossings. Almost treeless, the Outer Hebrides are composed of some of the world's oldest rock, which lies beneath a layer of peat carpeted with heather and grass. Here also are some of Britain's most attractive Atlantic beaches, backed by fertile coastal plains known as 'machair'. Everywhere are reminders of ancient islanders – cairns and tombs, forts and churches.

BARRA

Little Barra is a mere 5 miles (8 km) wide by 8 miles (12.9 km) long. You can reach it by ferry from Lochboisdale or Oban, arriving at the main settlement of Castlebay. The 11th-century castle in the harbour here, Kisimul, was a stronghold of the MacNeills, a ruffianly clan noted for their piratical raids on the shores of Northern Ireland – a boat will take you across on open days. Many visitors choose to fly in to Barra, however, landing on the long silvery beach of Traigh Mhor to the north of the island. It's the only beach in Britain that doubles as a runway for commercial flights (tides permitting). There are more splendid sandy beaches on the western side of the island. Gaelic culture thrives here – look out for the Barra Feis, a lively summer festival.

HARRIS AND LEWIS

Harris and Lewis are often assumed to be two islands, but they are one, linked by a narrow neck of land. Harris, to the south, is the gem of the Outer Isles, with an exceptionally beautiful, if subtle, landscape which has been the inspiration as well as a source of materials and dyes for the famous Harris weavers – roads are dotted

with signs inviting you to the cottage workshops.

The main village is Tarbert (*Tairbeart*), which is also the ferry terminal from Skye. The beaches and clear blue water here are magnificent. In the south, St Clement's Church houses some remarkable carvings; with the tomb of Alexander Macleod, they form the finest group of late medieval sculptures in the Western Isles. An T-ob, up the coast, was once known as Leverburgh. It was named after Lord Leverhulme, who purchased the islands in 1918 and did his best to encourage industry here.

The ruins of an old whaling station can be seen at Bunavoneadar. The large brick chimney seems incongruous in this landscape, but it is a reminder of the former importance of the whaling industry.

Lewis has great undulating blanket peat moors, hundreds of lochs and is inhabited by at least 750 weavers. Sabbath observance is taken very seriously here, so most places close on Sundays. The busy fishing port of Stornoway is the only town and the administrative centre. The woodlands of nearby Lews Castle were imported, with their earth, in the 19th century.

The Black House at Arnol is a traditional Hebridean dwelling open as a museum to illustrate the life of a crofting family. Further south along the coast is the ancient tower of Dun Carloway Broch, an Iron-Age dwelling which still stands about 30 feet (9.1m) high. South from here is Callanish, considered second only to Stonehenge in importance. Dating from between 5000 and 3000 BC, this site consists of 13 standing stones and an avenue of 19 monoliths. The impressive visitor centre explains its significance and the story of its rediscovery from beneath the peat in the 19th century.

The Standing Stones of Callanish may once have been used for sun worship

HARRIS TWEED

This famous cloth is made on treadle looms only on the island with two names – Lewis and Harris. It was Lady Dunmore, the wife of the Laird of the Islands, who introduced the cloth to the British aristocracy in the 1840s, thus providing the islanders with a way of making an income from their own skills. The Harris Tweed Authority states that 'Harris tweed must be made from 100 per cent pure virgin wool, dyed, spun and finished in the Outer Hebrides and hand woven by the islanders in their own homes.' Now fashion designers from Europe to Japan and the United States use the cloth, which is traditionally associated with sporting clothes. Always check for the famous Orb mark, the proof that a piece of cloth is authentic.

Neatly hung stones secure the roof of this croft house at Carinish, on North Uist

CORNCRAKES

It is rare on mainland Britain to hear the distinctive 'crek crek' sound of the corncrake, although this grassland bird was once much more widespread. Corncrakes need tall vegetation such as rough grass and iris beds between April and June to provide safe cover. Unfortunately their preferred hay field habitats on the mainland have been largely destroyed by intensive mechanised agriculture, which is thankfully not practised in the crofts of the Hebrides. These islands now hold most of the small relict British breeding population of these migratory birds, which spend their winters in Asia and Africa. See or hear them on the RSPB's Balranald Reserve.

NORTH UIST AND BENBECULA

The island of North Uist lies amid a scattering of smaller islands, with abundant lochans and magnificent white sandy beaches (especially around the north). Fertile lush green machair in the west rises to low mountains on the eastern side.

The main village and ferry terminal for the CalMac Ferry from Tarbert (Harris) and Uig (Skye) is Lochmaddy. From here you can explore the RSPB's Balranald Nature Reserve, at Hougharry (*Hogha Gearraidh*), with its small croft-house converted into an informative visitor centre. Originally created for the protection of the red-necked phalarope, the reserve is well worth a visit.

North of Sollas lies Udal, a highly specialised archaeological site reached by a windswept walk across the machair, where traces of 4,000 years of continuous habitation were covered by sand from 1697 until recent excavations. North Uist has a notable concentration of chambered cairns, and the best of these, at Barpa Langass, can be seen from the roadside. The melancholy ruin of Trinity Temple (*Teampull na Trionaid*), a medieval monastery near Carinish, is a former centre of learning for the sons of chiefs.

Benbecula, often described as a stepping stone between the Uists, has a causeway that spans the mesmerising mosaic of freshwater lochs, sea lochs, and sandbanks. This is an excellent place for birdwatching, a little fishing or simply relaxing in beautiful surroundings. There is a cave in the only prominent hill, Rueval, which is where Prince Charles Edward Stuart hid in 1746. It was from here, dressed as Betty Burke, that he travelled east to Rossinish Point and made his famous crossing to Skye and freedom, assisted by Flora Macdonald. The army base at Balivanich is a centre of activity on the island, and continues a long history of military activity beginning well before the Iron Age at Dun Gainhich (*Dunganachy*) which still has some of the original walls in place.

ST KILDA

One of only three World Heritage Sites in Scotland, this remote, rocky island some 110 miles (177km) from the mainland, is owned by the National Trust for Scotland, and co-managed with Scottish Natural Heritage. The village of Hirta was laid out in the 1830s. Corbelled stone structures used for storage and known as 'cliets' are scattered everywhere.

In the late 17th century there were about 180 inhabitants on the island, but by the 1880s nearly half the population had emigrated, leaving an ageing community behind. In 1930 the remaining islanders were evacuated. St Kilda was then uninhabited until the Ministry of Defence eventually established a base here in 1957.

SOUTH UIST

South Uist is the second largest island in the Outer Hebrides. With a wonderful 20-mile (32.2km) stretch of sandy beach in the west, backed by machair, and with mountains sprawling down the eastern side, South Uist is excellent walking country, especially with a pair of binoculars. At Loch Druidibeg National Nature Reserve corncrakes are frequent seasonal migrants, and there are greylag geese and a good many mute swans further north on Loch Bee. The area is excellent for salmon and trout fishing too.

Lochboisdale, in the south, is the main ferry port. Howmore, about halfway up the island, has the remains of a number of interesting medieval churches, bearing witness to the ancient ecclesiastical importance of these isolated islands. Near the youth hostel at Howmore lie the ruins of two chapels and two churches and the burial place of the chiefs of Clanranald, who ruled South Uist from the 1370s. Dedicated to St Mary, St Dugal and St Dermot, the churches were once linked with Caisteal Bheagram, a largely ruined castle on an island in neighbouring Loch an Eilean, which is today accessible only by boat. The local museum, recently refurbished, has information on all this, as well as the story of Flora MacDonald, whose ruined birthplace you can visit near by.

PEAT CUTTING

Beds of peat several metres thick have been laid down over thousands of years in the cold, damp, largely treeless and waterlogged areas of the highlands and islands. Temperatures below 5°C ensure that the heathers, mosses and bracken growing there do not decay as in warmer climates, but instead are compressed under their own weight in the absence of oxygen, to produce an organic, rich peat layer which can be burned as fuel for heating and cooking. 'Peats' are cut with special spades in the summer months by the crofters, whose ancient gathering rights are protected under Scots law. The peats are laid out to dry, and then stacked ready for the cold winter months.

The island of Eriskay can be seen off the southern tip of South Uist

The Hebrides

Leisure Information
Places of Interest
Shopping
The Performing Arts
Sports, Activities
and the Outdoors
Annual Events and Customs

Checklist ✓

Leisure Information

TOURIST INFORMATION CENTRES

INNER HEBRIDES
Broadford, Skye
(Seasonal). Tel: 01471 822361.
Portree, Skye
Bayfield House. Tel: 01478
612137.
OUTER HEBRIDES
Castlebay, Barra
Main Street (Seasonal).
Tel: 01871 810336.
Lochboisdale, South Uist
Pier Road (Seasonal). Tel: 01878
700286.
Lochmaddy, North Uist
Pier Road (Seasonal). Tel: 01876
500321.
Stornoway, Lewis
26 Cromwell Street. Tel: 01851
703088.
Tarbert, Harris
Pier Road (Seasonal). Tel: 01859
502011.

OTHER INFORMATION

Ferries
Caledonian MacBrayne Ferries
Ferry Terminal, Gourock. Tel:
01475 650100. For Hebrides via
Firth of Clyde, or west coast
ports; 'Rover' tickets available.
Western Ferries (Clyde), Hunters
Quay, Dunoon. Tel: 01369
704452.

Historic Scotland
Longmore House, Salisbury Pl,
Edinburgh. Tel: 0131 668 8800.
National Trust for Scotland
28 Charlotte Square, Edinburgh.
Tel: 0131 243 9300.
www.nts.org.uk
RSPB
Dunedin House, 25 Ravelston
Terrace, Edinburgh. Tel: 0131
311 6500. www.rspb.com
Scottish Tourist Board
23 Ravelston Terrace,
Edinburgh. Tel: 0131 332 2433.
www.visitscotland.com
Scottish Wildlife Trust
Cramond House, Cramond
Glebe Road, Edinburgh.
Tel: 0131 312 7765.
www.swt.org.uk
Weather
Weathercall for northwest
Scotland.
Tel: 09068 232795.

ORDNANCE SURVEY MAPS

Landranger 1:50,000 sheets 8,
13, 14, 18, 22, 23, 31, 32, 33,
39.
Outdoor Leisure 1:25,000 sheet
8.

Places of interest

There will be an admission
charge at the following places of
interest unless otherwise stated.

INNER HEBRIDES
RUM
Kinloch Castle
Boat from Mallaig. Tel: 01687
462037. Tours by arrangement.
SKYE
Aros Heritage Centre
Viewfield Road, Portree.
Tel: 01478 613649. Open all
year, daily.
**Armadale Castle Gardens
and Museum of the Isles**
Armadale. Tel: 01471
844305/844227.
Open Apr–Oct daily.
Borreaig Park
Dunvegan. Tel: 01470 511311.
Local history museum, also sells
bagpipes, silver, wool and other
local goods. Open all year, daily.
Colbost Folk Museum
3 miles (4.8km) west of
Dunvegan. Tel: 01470 521296.
Open Apr–Oct, daily.
**Dunvegan Castle and
Gardens**
Tel: 01470 521206. Open all
year, daily.
Kylerhea Otter Haven
North of Kylerhea. Open all
year, daily. Free.
Old Skye Crofter's House
Luib, 7 miles (11.2km) north-
west of Broadford. Tel: 01470
822427. Open all year, daily.
Skye Museum of Island Life
Hungladder, Kilmuir. Tel: 01470

552206. Open Apr–Oct
Mon–Sat.

OUTER HEBRIDES
BARRA
Cille Bharra
Eoligarry, north end of island.
Open all reasonable times. Free.
BENBECULA
Museum Sgoil Lionacleit
Four miles (6.4km) south of Baile
a'Mhanaich (Balivanich) on
B892. Tel: 01870 602684. Open
all year. Free.
HARRIS AND LEWIS
Black House
Arnol, 15 miles (24km) north
west of Stornoway. Tel: 0131
668 8800. Open all year, most
days. Closed Sun.
Callanish Standing Stones
Off A858 12 miles (19.2km)
west of Stornoway.
Tel: 0131 668 8800. Open at all
times. Free. Visitor Centre closed
Sun.
Dun Carloway Broch
A858, Carloway. Open all
reasonable times. Free. Visitor
Centre open Jun–Sep.
Tel: 01851 643338.
Gearrannan Village
A mile (1.6km) from bridge at
Carloway. Open all year, daily.
Museum Nan Eilean
Francis Street, Stornoway.
Tel: 01851 703773. Open all
year, most days. Free.
Ness Historical Society
Habost, Ness.
Tel: 01851 810377. Open daily
in summer.
**Steinacleit Cairn and Stone
Circle**
Loch an Duin, 12 miles (19.2km)
north of Stornoway.
Tel: 0131 668 8800. Open all
reasonable times. Free.
NORTH UIST
Taigh Tasgaidh
Lochmaddy Museum and Arts
Centre, Lochmaddy.
Tel: 01876 500293. Open all
year Mon–Sat.
Trinity Temple
Off the A865, 8 miles (12.8km)
south west of Lochmaddy. Open
all reasonable times. Free.
SOUTH UIST
South Uist Museum
Tel: 01878 710343. Open daily,
Apr–Oct.

SPECIAL INTEREST FOR
CHILDREN
The following places may be of
interest to visitors with children.
Unless otherwise stated there
will be an admission charge.

INNER HEBRIDES
SKYE
**Giant MacAskill Museum
Centre**
Dunvegan. Tel: 01470 521296.
Includes a life-size model of
Angus MacAskill, Scotland's
tallest man at 7 feet 9 inches
(2.3m). Open Apr–Oct, daily.
**Holmisdale House Toy
Museum**
Glendale. Tel: 01470 511240.
Open all year, most days.
Skye Serpentarium
The Old Mill, Harrapool,
Broadford. Tel: 01471 822209.
Open Easter–Oct, most days.

The Performing Arts

INNER HEBRIDES
SKYE
An Tuireann Arts Centre, Struan
Rd, Portree. Tel: 01478 613306.

Shopping

LOCAL SPECIALITIES

INNER HEBRIDES
SKYE
Distillery
Talisker Distillery, Carbost, on
B8009. Tel: 01478 640203.

OUTER HEBRIDES
BENBECULA
Paintings
Studio Gallery, Askernish.Tel:
01878 700237. Open Apr–Sep
most days, at other times by
appointment.
LEWIS
Pottery
Fear an Eich Coll Pottery, Back.
On B895 6 miles (9.6km) from
Stornoway. Tel: 01851 820219.

Sports, Activities and the Outdoors

ANGLING

There are ample opportunities
for angling. Enquire at local
Tourist Information Offices.

CYCLE HIRE
SKYE
Fairwinds Cycle Hire, Broadford.
Tel: 01471 822270.

GOLF COURSES
INNER HEBRIDES
SKYE
Isle of Skye Golf Club. Sconser.
Tel: 01478 650414.
OUTER HEBRIDES
LEWIS
Stornoway Golf Club, Lady Lever
Park. Tel: 01851 702240.

HORSE-RIDING
SKYE
Skye Riding Centre. Suledale, by
Portree. Tel: 01470 582419.

NATURE RESERVES
**Balranald Nature Reserve
(RSPB), North Uist**
Hougharry. Tel: 0131 311 6500
(head office).
**Loch Druidibeg National
Nature Reserve (RSPB),
South Uist**
Tel: 0131 311 6500 (head
office).

WATERSPORTS
SKYE
Dive and Sea the Hebrides.
Holidays for qualified divers. Tel:
01470 592219.
Whitewave, Skye's Outdoor
Centre, Uig (canoeing,
windsurfing). Tel: 01470
542414.

Annual Events and Customs

SKYE
Isle of Skye Highland Games,
early August.
Talisker Skye and Lochalsh Food
and Drink Festival, late
September.
BARRA
Feis Bharraidh – Isle of Barra
Festival, early July.

The checklists give details of just
some of the facilities within the
area covered by this guide.
Further information can be
obtained from Tourist
Information Centres.

Ross and Cromarty

The area of Ross and Cromarty sweeps across Scotland, embracing every landscape from the rugged, remote mountains and moorland of Assynt in the west to the rolling, fertile country of the Black Isle in the east. It is noted as a refuge for some of Scotland's native wildlife and as such it has some of the country's finest nature reserves. Ross and Cromarty are also also full of other surprises, including the sub-tropical gardens of Inverewe and the spa town of Strathpeffer, a delightful reminder of Victorian prosperity.

ALEXANDER MACKENZIE
In the graveyard of the parish church of Avoch, near Rosemarkie, lie the remains of the great Scottish explorer Sir Alexander Mackenzie (1755–1820). Mackenzie travelled to Canada in 1779 and was soon trading furs for the North West Company. Based at Fort Chipewyan on Lake Athabasca, he set out with a team of native Canadian Indians in 1789 to discover a route across the continent, but found instead a long river, which would be named after him, leading up to the Arctic Ocean. In 1793 he became the first white man to cross the Rockies and reach the Pacific.

The bulbous hill of Sgurr a'Chaorachain, near the pass of Bealach-na-Ba

APPLECROSS   Highland Map ref NG7144
Looking north from the picture-postcard village of Plockton, the rugged hills of Applecross fill both the view and the imagination. Until the last century this peninsula was almost as isolated as Knoydart. Rough tracks linked the old settlements along the coast down to Toscaig, and access from the south was via the breathtakingly spectacular Bealach-na-Ba, which reaches some 2,050 feet (624.8m). In 1965 a road was started around the northern margin from Shieldaig, making a pleasant circular route around this remote and beautiful place.

An Irish saint established a religious community here in the 7th century, but it was destroyed in a Viking raid. Today it is hard to believe that 3,000 people once thrived with their cattle in the green, fertile valley around the quiet village of Applecross itself – cleared from the land when the Mackenzies sold it off for a sporting estate; only the outlines of their deserted cottages remain.

BLACK ISLE Highland

The Black Isle is the fertile spit of land between the Cromarty and Moray Firths. The central forested ridge carries the peninsula's older name of Ardmeanach, and was part of lands gifted to her husband, Lord Darnley, by Mary, Queen of Scots.

Cromarty, on the northeastern tip of the peninsula, is a delightful 18th-century town, an important centre of fishing and commerce until the 19th century, when it was bypassed by the railways. The whitewashed Courthouse Museum ably tells the town's story. Hugh Miller, an eminent 19th-century geologist and writer who started life as a stonemason, lived in the little thatched cottage next door, now in the care of the National Trust for Scotland (see Walk on page 70). The fossil beach where he worked is 2 miles (3.2 km) away at Eathie.

Fortrose looks out across the Moray Firth. The cathedral was completed in the 15th century, but then unroofed in the 16th, before Cromwell plundered its great sandstone blocks to build the fortifications in Inverness. On the other side of the spit (once a popular spot for witch-burning but now dedicated to golf) lies Rosemarkie, notable for the Pictish remains displayed at the Groam House Museum and Pictish Centre.

The mud-flats of the Beauly Firth attract large numbers of birds – over-wintering greylag and pink-footed geese graze the fields around, and a variety of sea-ducks, including goldeneye and scoter, may be seen near the Kessock Bridge.

Evening light catches the impressive ruins of Fortrose Cathedral

DOLPHIN WATCH
Bottlenose dolphins found around the Scottish mainland are some of the largest in the world, and in the Moray Firth area there is one of only two resident populations in Britain, with at least 88 individuals identified. Cromarty has become the best place in Britain to see bottlenose dolphins in the wild – boat trips run by Dolphin Ecosse are available throughout the year (tel: 01381 7 600323 for details). There are also whale-watching trips during August and September.

Cromarty and the Moray Firth

A walk with excellent views of the Cromarty and Moray Firths, which are only surpassed by sightings of Scotland's only resident group of bottlenose dolphins. Paths can be muddy and overgrown; take a pair of binoculars. The walk can be shortened.

Time: 4½ hours. Distance: 6 miles (9.7km).
Location: On the A832 at Cromarty.
Start: Park in the car park in Forsyth Place.
(OS grid ref: NH788676.)
OS Map: Pathfinder 134 (Cromarty & Balintore)
1:25,000.
See Key to Walks on page 121.

ROUTE DIRECTIONS

From the car park turn left, then immediately right to walk along the coast for 220 yards (201m). Look for a sign for the Courthouse. Turn right up to the Cromarty Arms and the Courthouse, then left past **Hugh Miller's Cottage** to the Cromarty Historic Scottish Kirk. Turn left down Burnside Place, past the Cromarty Study Centre, a converted 18th-century brewery. Turn right at the sign 'South Sutor Viewpoint' along Miller Road, then turn right and go uphill. After the archway on the right, with the sign 'Private House', make a short detour left to a 17th-century graveyard.

Rejoin the road, heading up to the T-junction where a panorama of Nigg Bay and semi-submersible oil rigs in the Cromarty Firth can be seen. Turn right and then left, passing cottages on to a farm track. Pass through two gates in quick succession at the barn. Take the right-hand gate and walk through a wooded glade towards the coast until you see a stile at the bottom on the right.

Dolphins may be seen from here – look out for seagulls hovering over the sea, they may give away their position. From here you can venture along the top of the cliff, but this is not advisable for children. Descend to the beach (take care as the path is narrow) with its abandoned fishing huts, sea-stacks and natural arches, but beware of the tide. Return back up the path and over the stile. At this point you can shorten the walk by retracing the path back to Cromarty, or carry on and complete the walk through fields where there may be cattle, including bulls.

To continue, go back to the trees, turn right, go under a fence then walk straight ahead along the edge of the field to link up with a more obvious path. At the next fence turn left and walk uphill for 30 yards (27m) crossing

the right side of the gate on to the grass path around the headland, to another gate and a view of the seven counties/districts of the area: Caithness, Sutherland, Nairn, Ross and Cromarty, Inverness, Moray and Banff. Head downhill on a wide grassy path, through a gap in the fence to a final gate beyond and the old Coastguard Lookout Station. From here the path descends and links up with a metalled road. Continue to the T-junction, turn right and return to **Cromarty**.

POINTS OF INTEREST

Hugh Miller's Cottage
Built in 1711, the thatched cottage (National Trust for Scotland) is now a museum on the life of Hugh Miller, geologist, writer and editor, who was born here. His numerous books included *Scenes and Legends of Northern Scotland* (1835), and he recorded his findings in palaeontology and geology in *Old Red Sandstone*.

Moray Firth Dolphins
Over 100 bottlenose dolphins have been identified as residing in the Cromarty and inner Moray Firths. Up to 13 feet (4m) in length, they can live for 40 years, and are distinguished from porpoises by their grey skin, short noses and playful manner. They use distinctive sounds to communicate with each other, including a unique signature whistle. Harbour porpoises, minke whales, common and grey seals are also prevalent in the area. In 1982, a rare humpback whale was seen in the central Moray Firth.

Cromarty
The 18th-century seaport town has good examples of

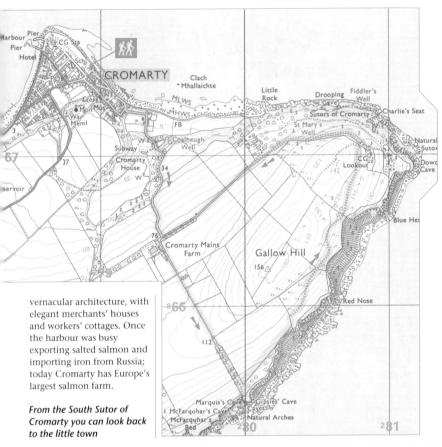

vernacular architecture, with elegant merchants' houses and workers' cottages. Once the harbour was busy exporting salted salmon and importing iron from Russia; today Cromarty has Europe's largest salmon farm.

From the South Sutor of Cromarty you can look back to the little town

GRUINARD

For many people, the name of Gruinard is irrevocably associated with the germ warfare tests of World War II, which were to contaminate the land for many years. In a controlled experiment in 1942 a number of bombs containing anthrax were detonated on the little island in the bay, and the results of the bacillus on a flock of sheep were closely observed. Needless to say, the sheep died horribly. Some 45 years later the island was cleaned up and declared safe. Today it is a beautiful, peaceful spot in a magnificent arc of a pink sandy bay.

The scattered settlement of Gairloch sprawls along this beautiful coast

GAIRLOCH   Highland Map ref NG8076

This popular holiday village with its excellent Heritage Museum is spread around a sunny, sandy bay, with the heights of the delightfully named Flowerdale looming behind. There are superb views out to the islands, and Gairloch lies at the heart of a fine scenic area which takes in the incomparable Loch Maree. West from the village, the road winds around the bay and eventually turns into a track, leading to the former lighthouse at Rubha Reidh. To the south of the bay there are intriguing woody inlets, perfect for exploring in a small boat. Beyond sheltered Badachro the road passes sandy bays to end at Redpoint, but energetic walkers can take the long path to Diabaig on Loch Torridon.

Behind Gairloch the A832 leads to the long stretch of water that is Loch Maree, famous for its fishing. It is surrounded by high mountains and scattered with darkly wooded islands. The highest peak on the northern shore is Slioch (3,219 feet/981m), while to the south Beinn Eighe, with its cap of white quartzite, lies at the heart of Britain's first National Nature Reserve – you can find out about nature trails and picnic spots at the visitor centre at Aultroy, towards the eastern end of the loch. Isle Maree, by Letterewe, was the site of a 7th-century hermitage, and may have had much older, druidical connections. Queen Victoria was enchanted with the whole area when she visited in 1877, giving her name to the waterfall near Talladale.

INVEREWE Highland Map ref NG8683

Surrounded by barren peatbogs, rocks and water lies Inverewe, one of Britain's most remarkable gardens, and a mecca for plant-lovers from all over the world. Lying on the same latitude as Moscow and Hudson's Bay, the site must have seemed a daunting challenge when Osgood MacKenzie inherited the Inverewe Estate in 1862. But a determined gardener is a force to be reckoned with, and Osgood possessed every quality necessary to create this wonderful oasis – imagination, vision, perseverance and patience.

First he planted a shelter belt of pines and firs, carted out the rocks and replaced them with hundreds of tonnes of garden soil. Once protected from the winds, Inverewe could benefit from the warming effects of the North Atlantic Drift. Rhododendrons were planted in profusion, and still provide one of the most spectacular attractions in the early summer. Paths meander between them and beneath the pines, and pass an almost bewildering array of rare and exotic plants, collected from all over the world. Rock gardens are bright with alpines, including many from New Zealand, and in the area called 'Japan' are tree ferns and palms.

There are wonderful views along the loch from the tip of the garden at Cuddy Rock, and also from in front of the house, built in 1937 after fire destroyed Osgood's original building. Mackenzie died in 1922, and his daughter Mairi, who had maintained and developed his vision, presented the garden to the National Trust for Scotland in 1952.

Tender plants flourish in the walled garden at Inverewe

FLOWER POTS TO POT SHOTS
Osgood Mackenzie, creator of Inverewe Garden, was a typical Victorian gentlemen when it came to sport. He was a keen shot and proud of his success. In 1856 alone he records bagging 1,900 head of game, including 184 hares, 110 golden plover, 91 rock pigeons, 35 wild duck, 53 snipe and 49 partridges, as well as 1,313 grouse – and this does not include roe deer, ptarmigan, teal and geese. He was anxious to protect his birds from what he called vermin, so he poisoned and trapped foxes, badgers, otters, polecats, pine martens and wildcats. In the course of four seasons he also disposed of 34 golden eagles. Though today we may look askance at such apparently indiscriminate slaughter, Mackenzie was not out of step with his times.

The Ancient Round House of Badachro

A pleasant walk taking in woodland, An Torr and an ancient site. Good views of Loch Gairloch, Badachro harbour and the distant mountains of Wester Ross can be seen before returning along the leafy river's edge. The first section has some uneven ground along the river that is not suitable for very young children or the elderly.

Time: 2 hours. Distance: 2 miles (3.2km).
Location: 6 miles (9.6km) southwest of Gairloch.
Start: Take the A832 south from Gairloch, turn right at the stone bridge over the River Kerry on to the B8056 signposted 'Red Point and Badachro'. After 3 miles (4.8km), passing Loch Bad a' Chrotha on the left, pull in and park on the right just before the old stone bridge.
(OS grid ref: NG785731.)
OS Maps: Pathfinder 128 (Loch Gairloch)
1:25,000.
See Key to Walks on page 121.

ROUTE DIRECTIONS

Go through the obvious gap in the fence at the end of the pull-in and follow the steep path above the fast-flowing Abhainn Bad a' Chrotha. Continue downhill (be careful of the steep incline on your left) and turn sharp right at a path junction opposite a small wooded island. The track ascends boggily through heather and myrtle to open moorland. To your right the summit cairn of An Torr comes into view. For views of **Loch Gairloch** and the mountains of Wester Ross, strike off right here across the rough grass and heather, on one of the many sheep trods which will lead you to within scrambling distance of the summit. Return to the main path and continue ascending until it levels out approaching the brow of the hill.

Turn left here, across rough heather on to a rocky ridge, which in 65 yards (60m) leads to a boulder balanced on a little crag by a clump of trees. Continue along the ridge with the river down to your left and also now straight ahead. As you come over the brow of a low rise you will see a path ahead of you, leading to a ring of heather covered boulders. These are the remains of one of ten **round houses** to be found around the slopes of An Torr.

Follow the path beyond the round house to a junction with a path running parallel with the river. Turn right and descend into the trees, following this path above the river until you reach a rocky cleft on the left. Clamber through this gully to emerge on a rocky outcrop facing the pier and outdoor centre in sheltered **Badachro Bay**.

Retrace your steps, following the path up through the woods. By the hut cirlce keep straight on, taking the path that re-enters the **birch woodland** with the river down to your right. Follow this, often boggy, path upstream enjoying the riverside views as you return to the starting point.

POINTS OF INTEREST

Loch Gairloch
The loch, although popular for sailing and fishing, is far from crowded. The area was once famous for spring cod-fishing. Today, common fish like haddock and mackerel are caught here, but the fishermen sometimes catch the more unusual small octopus and cuckoo wrasse. Small boats are available for hire, or there are skippered fishing boats; alternatively, yacht cruises set sail from the nearby harbours. The Gairloch Heritage Museum is the place to discover the history of the local fishing industry. Exhibits include examples of typical fishing boats that have been used in the Loch Gairloch area.

Round House 'Hut Circles'
Bronze- and Iron-Age hut circles of this kind are scattered all over Wester Ross. Their roofs were supported by a ring of wooden posts, the walls were likely to have been of made of wicker and the whole structure thatched with vegetation.

Badachro Bay
This is a typical Wester Ross fishing village, with an old jetty ramp leading down to the unusually shaped bay and the islands of Eilean Tioram, Sgeir Ghlas and

Looking over sheltered Badachro Bay from An Torr

Eilean Horrisdale. The bay is colourful with heather which reaches down to the sea shore, where the rocks are covered with lichen and fringed with orange seaweed.

Birch Woodland
Wood from the local birch trees was an adaptable commodity. It was burnt to smoke herrings or used to build furniture and make tools and brooms. Later it was also turned to make cotton reels. The bark was useful for tanning and for house insulation, and birch was also turned into charcoal for iron smelting. The cotton grass found around Badachro was used for candlewicks and to stuff the pillows of the villagers.

Gairloch to Ullapool

This is a magnificent 50-mile (80.5km) linear drive, along the superb mountainous coastline of north-west Scotland, with plenty of viewpoints along the route.

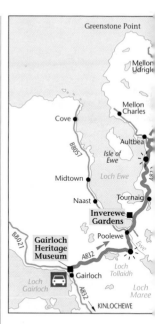

ROUTE DIRECTIONS

See Key to Car Tours on page 120.

The drive starts at **Gairloch Heritage Museum**, a converted farmstead which depicts the way of life in this West Highland parish, from Stone-Age times to the present day. It includes a Pictish inscribed stone, a reconstructed croft house room, and geology, archaeology, agriculture and fishing sections. From the museum take the A832 signposted 'Poolewe'. Continue on this road passing Loch Tollaidh, with freshwater fish farm cages on the right, until you arrive at magnificent freshwater Loch Maree. Pull in at the unmarked viewpoint on the left to admire the scenery.

Drive on, passing through Poolewe – a favourite holiday place – and on to **Inverewe Gardens** some 8 miles (12.8km) from Gairloch. To visit these unique gardens, park in the car park on the left (there are also views of Loch Ewe from here). Inverewe Gardens, owned by The National Trust for Scotland, was created over a century ago by Osgood Mackenzie, and his daughter, Mairi Sawyer, continued the work. Originally a windswept rocky and peaty moorland, with only two small trees, it is now one of Europe's most exotic visual extravaganzas. Taking advantage of its shoreline position and of the Gulf

Stream climate, it now has over 2,500 species, including Himalayan lilies, Japanese hydrangeas, New Zealand shrubs and giant South Pacific forget-me-nots. There is also a walled garden and Victorian glasshouses.

Continue on the A832, passing on the left a viewpoint from which you can see the Isle of Ewe and an impressive military pier. Continue, passing on the left the minor road to the old crofting townships of Aultbea and Mellon Charles. Continue to Laide and turn left before the garage, toilets and post office to the ruined chapel, believed to have been founded by Columba's monks, and a viewpoint (not signed). From here there are magnificent views across Gruinard Bay to Gruinard Island, known for its germ warfare (anthrax) experiments in 1942. The island has since been pronounced clear, and was recently reinhabited.

Return to the main road and continue on the A832 around the bay and over the headland to the viewpoint just before Badcaul, from where there are views over Little Loch Broom to Beinn Ghobhlach and, to the right, the mountain of Sail Mhor. Follow the road along Little Loch Broom, passing rectangular mussel rafts and later fish cages before you reach Ardessie. The square and circular cages are the salt

water stage of the salmon-farming process. At Ardessie you pass a waterfall on the right. Continue, passing the war memorial, to Dundonnell Hotel from where you can see the magnificent tidal flats exposed at low water where wildfowl often feed.

The road, lined with Scots pine, follows the Dundonnell River and a series of lovely waterfalls. Continue ahead and where the road bears right and on the bend near Sìdhean na Sròine pull in to view of Loch Broom, with lush fields filling the valley floor – reputedly one of the most spectacular roadside views in Scotland. A little further on, at **Corrieshalloch Gorge**, pull in to the car park and go down to the suspension bridge to view the gorge. This is one of the most magnificent sights in the northwest; the gorge is a mile (1.6km) long and 200 feet (60m) wide, and was formed by glacial meltwaters. The **Falls of Measach** here are 150 feet

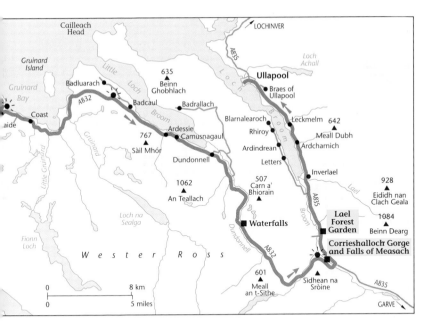

(46m) high.

Continue on the A832 until you reach a T-junction. Turn left on to the A835 (T) towards Ullapool, passing another entrance to the gorge on the left. Continue on the A835, passing **Lael Forest Garden** on your right, descending towards the lush pasture land, with sheep and drystone walls on your left. The road continues with Loch Broom on the left (notice the many crofts on the opposite side of the loch) into Ullapool and the end of the drive. Ullapool, on Loch Broom, is the largest town in Wester Ross and the main ferry link to Stornoway and the Outer Hebrides. This provides its main source of income since the decline of the local fishing industry, which once attracted 'Klondyker' factory ships from Eastern Europe.

Rounding the valley at the head of Loch Broom

THE CURSE OF CALDA HOUSE
Near the ruins of the MacLeods' 15th-century Ardvreck Castle on the shores of Loch Assynt you can see the remains of a fine mansion. This was Edderchalder, or Calda House, many-chambered and at least two storeys high, built around 1720 by the up-and-coming Mackenzies. Legend has it that the unfortunate woman who lived there was a witch and had cursed the district in a fit of rage, so that crops failed. Around 1737, after yet another miserable harvest, the curse was only lifted when the house was struck by a righteous bolt of lightning. Like the house, the castle was also destroyed by fire.

From the Knockan Visitor Centre the distinctive peak of Suilven can be seen to the right of Cul Mor

INVERPOLLY   Highland Map ref NC1412

North of Ullapool the habitation is sparse and the landscape becomes altogether bigger and wilder, with giant, bare mountains looming out of bleak, bitter moorland. The Inverpolly National Nature Reserve, managed by Scottish Natural Heritage, offers access to this fine, dramatic countryside in all its glory, and the visitor centre at Knockan is a good place to start. The diversity of habitats in the region is revealed, including bogs, lochs and patches of ancient woodland, with a corresponding diversity of flora. A geology trail here illuminates the formation of the Assynt area, and part of the 'Moine Thrust' can be seen in the rocks of Knockan Cliff. There are excellent views from the top of the mountains of Coigach. Of these, Stac Pollaidh (2,008 feet/612m) is the most popular, and a relatively easy walk leads up from the minor road by Loch Lurgainn. Look out for deer and birds of prey, and you may even see signs of wildcats in the area. To the north on a clear day you can see the familiar form of Suilven (2,402 feet/732m), but this peak is strictly for experienced mountaineers.

There is a further extensive nature reserve at Inchnadamph. From here the road leads round the shores of Loch Assynt, past the ruins of Ardvreck Castle, where the great soldier Montrose was held prisoner in 1650. Beyond that is the popular angling centre of Lochinver (this links up with a narrow but very scenic road from Loch Lurgainn). Up the coast, just north of the hamlet of Clachtoll, there are the circular remains of a broch to be seen on the shoreline, dating back to the first century AD.

SHIELDAIG AND TORRIDON Highland Map ref NG8154/NG9055

The villages around Loch Torridon are picturesque, but cannot compete with the grandeur of some of the finest mountain scenery in Scotland. The road east from Shieldaig, a whitewashed, 18th-century planned village overlooking the pine-clad Shieldaig Island, gives views over Upper Loch Torridon to the huge mountain mass dominated by what Queen Victoria called 'that extraordinary mountain, Ben Liathach.'

Of red Torridonian sandstone, 750 million years old and 3,339 feet (1,024m) high, Liathach has a row of seven peaks topped with shining white quartzite from 150 million years later. It forms part of the National Trust for Scotland's 16,100-acre (6,520ha) Torridon Estate. The Trust's Countryside Centre in Torridon village can advise on the best routes in the mountains, but guided walks are recommended if you want to tackle the 5-mile (8km) ridge between Liathach's peaks.

The Deer Museum near by has a herd of wild deer, and lots of information about their life on the hills. Further on, Beinn Eighe presents a forbidding face to the traveller, but like the other mountains has impressive corries to the north. Britain's first National Nature Reserve was established here to protect the remnant of the native Caledonian pine forest on its slopes.

The road north of Loch Torridon, with wonderful views over to the Applecross peninsula, passes through Fasag, built to house families displaced in the clearances, and several crofting settlements to end at Lower Diabaig, from where you can walk to Redpoint, far out on the coast of Wester Ross.

MOUNTAIN MOGGIES
The hills of Torridon are home to many species, but the wildcats are among the most elusive. They live on the loneliest and most remote mountain sides, hunting at night for small animals and birds, though they have been known to take lambs and young deer, too. Pure-bred wildcats have litters in May, and are bigger than domestic cats, to which they are only distantly related. Their yellowy-grey fur is prominently striped in black, and they have thick, bushy tails. Around 24 inches (61cm) from nose to tail, they can be awesomely fierce, spitting and growling when roused, though they purr, like any cat, when contented. It is not always easy to recognise a pure wildcat, as so many have interbred with feral domestic cats.

Enjoying an eagle's-eye view to the red ridge of Liathach, high above Torridon village

The delightful spa town of Strathpeffer

VITRIFIED FORTS

Vitrified Iron-Age hill forts are found throughout Scotland, Ireland and continental Europe. Vitrification occurred when the wooden beams used in the construction of stone ramparts were set on fire by an attacking enemy – the intense heat could cause certain softer rocks to melt and re-fuse in great lumps on cooling. Knock Farril, above Strathpeffer, is a particularly good example; another is Craig Phadrig, set on a prominent hilltop to the west of Inverness.

STRATHPEFFER   Highland Map ref NH4858

Once hailed as 'the Harrogate of the North', Strathpeffer is a curious phenomenon to find above the Highland line – a genteel, attractive little spa town, complete with Victorian architectural twirls such as verandahs and ornamental barge-boards. Locals had known about the curative properties of the mineral springs here for centuries, but thanks to the serious scientific analysis of the water in 1819, Strathpeffer became a boom town. The first pump room opened the following year, and visitors flocked to fill the new hotels and villas. While never perhaps in the same league as Bath, the town did attract royalty from overseas, and the railway had to be specially extended from Dingwall to cater for the number of visitors – at the height of its fame there were even through-trains from London.

Inevitably, tastes changed, and Strathpeffer's popularity declined after World War II. Many of the spa buildings have disappeared, and the old wooden railway station now houses crafts and visitor centres, but the Pump Room remains and has been restored. The town offers excellent golfing and recreational facilities to its visitors. Don't miss the Pictish stone slab, set in a field near the station. Deeply carved with an inverted, patterned horseshoe shape above a standing eagle, its original purpose is unknown.

There are several good places to walk here, including the ridge of Knock Farril to the south (see Walk on page 82), and through the woods to the Falls of Rogie to the west. Salmon may be seen in the Blackwater River here, and there are pleasant picnic sites between the trees.

ULLAPOOL   Highland Map ref NH1294

As you approach on the A835, the little whitewashed town of Ullapool is neatly laid out before you on a spit of land curving into the waters of Loch Broom. The tidy grid-plan of the streets reveals that this is a model town, and indeed it was laid out to a plan developed by the British Fishery Society in 1788. The site was carefully chosen to provide a good harbour for the fishing, and to squeeze out the Dutch herring vessels which had been taking full advantage of the lack of local boats. The great Thomas Telford had a hand in the design, but the herring did not last, and, without the lifeline of the railway, the settlement declined. The Fishery Society had chosen their site well, however, and in the first half of the 20th century boats came over from the east coast and fortunes revived. Until the mid-1990s, the local economy was given a boost by the distinctive 'Klondyker' factory ships from Eastern Europe, processing the catches of east coast trawlermen in the loch's sheltered waters. But the collapse of the Russian economy saw them disappear and now tourism is the main industry.

Ullapool is the gateway to the remote northwestern tip of Scotland, as well as the main ferry port for Stornoway. The broad streets are well worth exploring and there's a good little museum. Around the coast at Achiltibuie is the Hydroponicum, a scientific delight, where bananas and other exotic plants thrive without the benefit of soil – it is open through the summer, and seeing is believing! At the head of Loch Broom, don't miss the dramatic Corrieshalloch Gorge, and the suspension bridge just below the Falls of Measach.

THE SUMMER ISLES

This little group of islands lies just off the coast, some 12 miles (19.3km) northwest of Ullapool, and is well worth a visit if you enjoy peace and quiet – seals and seabirds are the chief inhabitants.

Naturalist Fraser Darling lived on Tanera More and wrote his *Island Years* here. Today, fish-farming has replaced fish-curing as the main support for the islands.

Ullapool's grid pattern of streets was planned in the 18th century

Knock Farril Fort and The Eagle Stone

A spectacular walk to a vitrified fort, views of Loch Ussie and a fine Pictish stone. A gentle hill climb on clear paths.

Time: 3½ hours. Distance: 5 miles (8km).
Location: Strathpeffer.
Start: From the Tourist Information Centre in Strathpeffer drive up the hill and turn left in front of the youth hostel; drive down the wooded lane, turn right and park in the car park.
(OS grid ref: NH481573.)
OS Map: Pathfinder 159 (Dingwall & Strathpeffer) 1:25,000.
See Key to Walks on page 121.

ROUTE DIRECTIONS

The entrance to **Blackmuir Wood** is marked by a green post with a footprint and viewpoint symbol. Walk round the edge of the lochan and turn left by some wooden chalets. Turn immediately right and follow the sign 'Forest Walk'. Follow posts with green and blue bands until you see fields on the left. Cross a plank bridge. On the left is a stile and a path leading down the field – remember this point for the return journey.

Follow the sign to the Touchstone Maze. Keeping the maze on your right, follow the path uphill until it intersects a broad path; turn left and keep straight ahead. Go through the gate at the end of the forest and continue until the path divides, taking the right track which swings uphill on to a flat area between the ridges.

Turn left up towards the grass-covered ruins of **Knock Farril Fort**, and the magnificent views of Dingwall, the Cromarty Firth. Return to the flat area beneath the fort. Do not follow the original path, but head uphill over the facing hog's-back ridge for views of Loch Ussie and Strathpeffer.

At the end of the ridge ignore the sharp right turn and go through the gate. Turn right, downhill into the woods, following the sign to Strathpeffer. Cross one track and turn left at the next. After about 66 yards (60m), turn right down to the Touchstone Maze and along to the stile referred to earlier in this walk. Cross over the stile into the field, and continue until a steep road takes you to the Ben Wyvis Hotel.

Follow the signs for the **Eagle Stone**, cross the road (A834), turn left, then right and continue until you reach a leafy lane. Halfway down the lane turn left through a gap in the hedge to see the Pictish stone and the distant view of Knock Farril. Go back down the lane and return to the main road. Turn right and walk past the Victorian Station Visitor Centre with its Museum of Childhood, the Spa Tea Room and the Tourist Information Centre. Follow the road through **Strathpeffer** uphill to the Youth Hostel, turn left and return to the car park at the start of the walk.

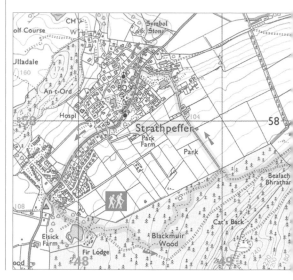

POINTS OF INTEREST

Blackmuir Wood
Managed by the Forest Enterprise, the wood contains mostly conifers, but also birch, rowan and bird cherry.

Touchstone Maze
Although a modern construction, dated 1992, the maze was built

incorporating alignments with the sun and moon, with a labyrinth pathway. It is constructed from all the major rock types of the Highlands and Islands of Scotland, with a display to identify them, and includes the Lewisian rocks of the Outer Hebrides and west coast which are over 3,000 million years old.

Knock Farril Fort
This Iron-Age fort (800–500 BC) is the best example of a vitrified fort in the north of Scotland. Vitrified literally means 'turned to glass'. The walls were set alight with extra wood between the stone, the intense heat melting the rocks and fusing them together. The result resembles slag with distinctive bubbles and flow marks. It isn't known whether this was done by

Strathpeffer lies cradled in a rolling green valley, seen here from the ridge of Knock Farril

defenders of the fort or by victorious attackers.

The Eagle Stone
The 7th-century Pictish stone with a carved eagle is possibly a memorial to a chief, a territorial marker or a symbol of a marriage alliance. The stone's name *Clach an Tiompan*, means 'sounding stone' or 'stone on the ground'. Local folklore suggests that if the stone falls over three times the valley floor will flood. It has fallen over twice, so far.

Strathpeffer
Britain's most northerly spa town, Strathpeffer's first pump room was built in about 1820, after sulphur and chalybeate springs were discovered. Hordes of visitors descended on the town from as far afield as London, after a pavilion, a rheumatic hospital and hotels were established.

Ross and Cromarty

✓ Checklist

Leisure Information
Places of Interest
Shopping
Sports, Activities
and the Outdoors
Annual Events and Customs

Leisure Information

TOURIST INFORMATION CENTRES

Gairloch
Auchtercairn. Tel: 01445 712130.
Lochcarron
Main Street (Seasonal).
Tel: 01520 722357.
North Kessock
Tel: 01463 731505.
Strathpeffer
The Square (Seasonal).
Tel: 01997 421415.
Ullapool
West Shore Street. Tel: 01854 612135.

OTHER INFORMATION

Ferries
Caledonian MacBrayne Ferries.
Ferry Terminal, Gourock.
Tel: 01475 650100. For
Hebrides via Firth of Clyde, or
west-coast ports; sailings to 23
islands. 'Rover' tickets available.
Forest Enterprise
Forestry Commision, 231
Corstorphine Road, Edinburgh.
Tel: 0131 334 0303.
Historic Scotland
Longmore House, Salisbury
Place, Edinburgh. Tel: 0131 668
8800.
National Trust for Scotland
28 Charlotte Square, Edinburgh.

Tel: 0131 243 9300.
www.nts.org.uk
RSPB
Dunedin House, 25 Ravelston
Terrace, Edinburgh. Tel: 0131
311 6500. www.rspb.com
Scottish Tourist Board
23 Ravelston Terrace,
Edinburgh. Tel: 0131 332 2433.
www.visitscotland.com
Scottish Wildlife Trust
Cramond House, Cramond
Glebe Road. Edinburgh. Tel:
0131 312 7765.
www.swt.org.uk
Weather
Weathercall for northwest
Scotland. Tel: 09068 232795.
Mountainall for West Highlands
Tel: 09068 500441.
Born to Climb Tel: 09015
600111.
Mountaincall for East Highlands
Tel: 09068 500442.

ORDNANCE SURVEY MAPS

Landranger 1:50,000 sheets 15,
16, 19, 20, 21, 24, 25, 26, 33,
34.
Outdoor Leisure 1:25,000 sheet
8.

Places of Interest:

There will be an admission
charge at the following places of
interest unless otherwise stated.

Achiltibuie Hydroponicum
Achiltibuie. 26 miles (41.8km)
north-west of Ullapool.
Tel: 01854 622202. Robert
Irvine's garden of the future,
growing plants without soil.
Open Easter–Sep, daily. Tours
on the hour 10–5; Oct Mon–Fri
tours 12 and 2.
Black Isle Brewery
Old Allangrange, Munlochy.
Tel: 01463 811871.
Free tours of independent
organic brewery in an 18th-
century house. Open most
days.
Countryside Centre
North of Torridon, off A896.
Tel: 01445 791221.
Audio-visual presentation on
scenery and wildlife.
Open: centre May–Sep; estate
and deer museum all year
daily.
Cromarty Courthouse
Church Street, Cromarty.
Tel: 01381 600418. Open
Easter–Oct daily.
Gairloch Heritage Museum
Gairloch. Tel: 01445 712287.
Open Apr–Sep most days; Oct
mornings only.
**Groam House Museum and
Pictish Centre**
High Street, Rosemarkie.
Tel: 01381 620961. Open
May–Oct most days.

Hugh Miller's Cottage
Church Street, Cromarty.
Tel: 01381 600245. Open
May–Sep daily.

Inverewe Gardens
On A832 at Poolewe, 6 miles
(9.6km) northeast of Gairloch.
Tel: 01445 781200. Open all
year, daily. Visitor Centre, shop
and restaurant mid-Mar to Oct
daily.

**Leckmelm Shrubbery and
Arboretum**
On A835, 3 miles (4.8km) south
of Ullapool. Open Apr–Sep,
daily. Honesty box.

Ullapool Museum
7–8 West Argyll Street. Tel:
01854 612987. Open Apr–Sep
daily, limited winter opening.

*Shieldaig's trim little
houses straggle along
the sheltered bay*

The following places may be of
interest to visitors with children.
Unless otherwise stated there
will be an admission charge.

**Black Isle Wildlife and
Country Park**
Drumsmittal, North Kessock.
Tel: 01463 731656. Open
Mar–Nov, daily.

**Highland Museum of
Childhood**
The Old Station, Strathpeffer.
Tel: 01997 421031.
Open Apr–Oct, most days.

Shopping

LOCAL SPECIALITIES

Crafts
The Studio, in the centre of
Achnasheen, by the railway
station. Jewellery workshop and
gallery. Tel: 01445 720227.

Open Apr–Sep, daily; Oct–Feb
most days.

Distilleries
Glen Ord Distillery Visitor
Centre, off the A832 on the
outskirts of Muir of Ord.
Tel: 01463 871334 for opening
times. Guided tours.
Glenmorangie Distillery Visitor
Centre, 1 mile (1.6km) from
Tain on the A9 towards Wick.
Tel: 01862 892477. Guided
tours, it is advisable to book in
advance.

Haggis
George Cockburn and Sons, 19
Mill Street, Dingwall. Tel: 01349
862315.

Smoked Products
Achiltibuie Smokehouse, at
Altandhu, 5 miles (8km) west of
Achiltibuie, north west of
Ullapool. Tel: 01854 622353.
Open Easter–Oct weekdays only,
but also Sat in high season.

Stoneware
Highland Stoneware, Mill Street, Ullapool. Also at Lochinver. Tel: 01571 844376 (Lochinver); 01854 612980 (Ullapool).

Sports, Activities and the Outdoors

ANGLING

There are ample opportunities for angling of all kinds in the area. Enquire at local Tourist Information Offices.

BOAT TRIPS

Moray Firth
Dolphin Ecosse. Tel: 01381 600323. Trips to see Dolphins; 2½ hours duration. Must be booked in advance. Also whale-watching trips Aug–Sep.

Summer Isles
Cruises from Achiltibuie. Tel: 01854 622200/622315. Rock formations, seals and bird-life.

COUNTRY PARKS, FORESTS AND NATURE RESERVES

Beinn Eighe National Nature Reserve
Kinlochewe. Tel: 01445 760254 (Scottish National Heritage office). Visitor centre open Apr–Sep. Free.

Inverpolly National Nature Reserve
At Knockan Cliff, off the A835, 12 miles (19.2km) northeast of Ullapool. Tel: 01854 613418.

Lael Forest Garden
On the A835 south of Ullapool. Two signposted car parks. Various waymarked walks through the forest with a forest garden of interesting trees from Britain and abroad. (Forest Enterprise)

Torridon Estate
Tel: 01445 791221. A 16,000-acre reserve in the Torridon Hills (NTS).

CYCLING

Contact Dornoch Forest Enterprise. Tel: 01862 810359.

GOLF COURSES

Alness
Alness Golf Club, Ardross Road. Tel: 01349 883877.

Fortrose
Fortrose Golf Club, Ness Road East. Tel: 01381 620529.

Gairloch
Gairloch Golf Club. Tel: 01445 712407.

Lochcarron
Lochcarron Golf Club, East End. Tel: 01520 766211.

Muir of Ord
Muir of Ord Golf Club, Great North Road. Tel: 01463 870825.

Portmahomack
Tarbat Golf Course. Ten miles (16km) east of Tain off the A9. Tel: 01862 871598.

Tain
Tain Golf Club, Golf Links. Tel: 01862 892314.

Finding time for a relaxed picnic in spectacular Glen Torridon

HORSE-RIDING

Tain
Northwilds Riding Centre, Fendom by Tain. Tel: 01862 892468.

WATERSPORTS

Muir of Ord
Fairburn Activity Centre (canoeing). Tel: 01997 433397.

Annual Events and Customs

Fortrose
St Boniface Fair, August.

Dingwall
Highland Traditional Music Festival, late June/early July. Dingwall Highland Games, mid-July.

Muir of Ord
Black Isle Show, early August.

Plockton
Plockton Regatta, late July to early August.

The checklists give details of just some of the facilities within the area covered by this guide. Further information can be obtained from Tourist Information Centres.

Caithness and Sutherland

The wide expanses of central Sutherland form one of the few wilderness areas remaining in western Europe, and their conservation is a matter of worldwide concern. Moor, bog and mountain support a rich diversity of plantlife which can be studied at the heart of the Flow Country, or at the extreme geographical points of Cape Wrath and Dunnet Head. Settlement is mostly confined to the coastal areas, with the fishing communities of the west, pleasant holiday places such as Golspie and historic towns like Thurso.

BETTYHILL   Highland Map ref NC7061

Lying beside a rocky bay on Scotland's inhospitable, wave-battered northern coast, the village of Bettyhill is linked for ever with the infamous Elizabeth, 1st Duchess of Sutherland, whose name it bears. With her husband and the hated factor, Patrick Sellar, the Duchess was prominent in the clearing of Sutherland's fertile land, evicting tenant crofters and replacing them with sheep. The scheme caused great hardship across the Highlands, and many were forced to emigrate in the clearances of 1814 and 1819. The green valley of Strathnaver, which runs south from Bettyhill to Syre and southwest to Altnaharra, once supported some 64 *clachans* and little townships; today it is eerily deserted. The Strathnaver Museum, east of Bettyhill, tells of those times and of the families who scraped a living along this wild shore.

Beside the road to Skelpick is a chain of prehistoric burial mounds, and Farr churchyard contains a carved slab cross from the 9th century. Today people come for the fishing and the landscape, or to trace the history of their dispossessed forebears.

THE UNQUIET GRAVE

In the churchyard at Farr you must look hard to find the fallen obelisk which commemorates the Reverend David MacKenzie. MacKenzie was the Duchess's man, given the unenviable task of serving the first eviction notices in 1814, and later assuring her ladyship that her tenants were happily resettled after the burning of their homes, despite evidence of great hardship and suffering. MacKenzie attempted to make amends in a letter to the estate in 1818, but his life was tainted, and his tomb is said to be cursed, for the stone will not stay upright. Old memories die hard in the Highlands.

The inhospitable shoreline at Farr, by Bettyhill

A TALE OF TWO BRIDGES
Today a bridge carries the A9 safely over the narrows of the Dornoch Firth, but until recently travellers relied on a boat to carry them between Ferrytown and Ferry Point on Cambuscurie Bay. Tragedy struck one night in 1809 when the ferry, overladen with revellers fresh from the market at Tain, capsized and sank; 70 lives were lost. The causeway bridge on the A9 north of Dornoch, across the head of Loch Fleet, replaced an old ferry crossing in 1815, and was designed by Thomas Telford.

Dornoch boasts an attractive little cathedral

DORNOCH   Highland Map ref NH7989

At the wide mouth of the Dornoch Firth, the dignified town of Dornoch is a popular holiday resort with great beaches, a lively craft centre and a world-class championship golf course. The modern course is described as 'very challenging', but golf has been taken seriously here since 1616, when monks from the local community started playing. In a garden down by the links stands the Witch's Stone, marking the demise of Janet Horne in 1722, who was tarred and feathered before being burned at the stake for turning her daughter into a pony and other devilish practices.

A royal burgh, the town was formerly important as the seat of the Bishops of Caithness. Their castle is now a comfortable hotel which shot to fame as the venue for Madonna's marriage to Guy Ritchie. Their son Rocco was christened in the tiny 13th-century cathedral. Burned down in the 16th century, it was finally rebuilt around 1835, with funds provided by the unpopular Elizabeth, Duchess of Sutherland. At Skelbo, north of Dornoch, a good forest walk takes you past the remains of an ancient broch.

DURNESS Highland Map ref NC4068

The odd little settlement of Durness is about as far as you can drive into the wild northwest corner of Scotland, but it is not quite the end of the road. The hamlet of Balnakeil lies a bit further north on the fertile Faraid peninsula and marks the site of the former radar station which was abandoned in the 1960s. Taken over by the local community, the old prefabricated buildings now contain a crafts centre. Gaelic scholars may come in search of the grave of the 18th-century poet Rob Donn, and golfers may fancy a game on the mainland's remotest golf course, but most visitors are drawn here by the lure of Cape Wrath. To visit the cape you must catch the summer ferry from neighbouring Keodale and take a minibus across the desolate, boggy moorland (the Royal Navy use it as a firing range) to reach the top. There's not a lot to see there, except a lonely lighthouse perched high on the cliffs, but chill winds and the roar of the pounding waves remind you that there are only the Faroe Islands between you and the Arctic. On a clear day you can see for miles from this point – as far as the Outer Hebrides and even Orkney. Britain's highest cliffs are along here, at Clo Mor (918 feet/280m), and offshore stacks support a famous colony of gannets.

Between Durness and the long, deep inlet of Loch Eriboll, Smoo Cave is well worth exploring. The name 'Smoo' derives from 'Smuga' – a hole or hiding place. A steep path leads down to the cavern, where the high arched mouth opens into three great chambers. There are watery pools within the cave, and dripping limestone has created a Gothic collection of stalactites and stalagmites. Sir Walter Scott started the tourist trail here in 1814, when the cave could only be approached from the sea.

The gaping mouth of Smoo Cave is approached today by a long flight of steps

WHAT'S IN A NAME?

The dramatic, angry seas hitting the reefs and cliffs around Cape Wrath suggest that this most northwesterly point of Britain is particularly well named. However, Wrath is probably taken from the Norse word 'hvarth', a turning point, and would have been a significant landmark on Viking trading routes around the coast. For pilots and seafarers it is still a familiar turning point, though thoughts of the wrath of the sea can never be far away.

Rosal Clearance Village, Sutherland

Starting alongside the River Naver, famous for its salmon, the clearly marked path through the forest leads to Rosal Clearance Village, which played an important, but tragic, part in Scotland's history. An easy walk on a well-signposted path.

Time: 1¼ hours. Distance: 2¼ miles (3.6km).
Location: 12 miles (19.2km) south of Bettyhill.
Start: From the Clearance Museum in the Old Church at Bettyhill take the A836 south. Turn left on to the B871 signposted 'Syre 9 miles'. Cross over the bridge at Syre and turn immediately right on to the Forest Enterprise track signposted 'Rosal Township'. After a mile (1.6km) turn left into the car park.
(OS grid ref: NC691427.)
OS Map: Pathfinder 64 (Mid Strathnaver) 1:25,000.
See Key to Walks on page 121.

ROUTE DIRECTIONS

Go through the large gate and follow the flat wide track through the Naver forestry plantation of Scots pine, **lodgepole pine** and larch planted in the early 1960s. Cross the Allt Rosail, a small stream, pass a large creosoted shed with a felt roof and continue until you reach the sign to **Rosal Village**. Turn left into a clearing in the centre of the forest, then go right and over the duck-boards. The first cairn describes the clearance of the Rosal township which was excavated by Glasgow University. Go through the gate and follow the white arrows. The walk depicts the life of the pre-clearance inhabitants through a series of interpretative boards.

Continue uphill to the next cairns which describe the traditional long houses which were built of stone, peat bog pine and heather. Follow the path to the boards describing the people, their animals and their crops, and pass a souterrain (an underground chamber) cairn of graded stones. Walk over marshy ground on duck-boards and

stepping stones to the cairn on the highest point on the site, and the echo point. Stop here for a few moments to enjoy the panorama then turn around to face the forest and shout into the trees to find the natural echo which bounces back off Beinn Rosail (853 feet/260m).

Continue on, now downhill, and fork left to a cairn at the edge of the forest. Follow the path which now bears to the right along the boundary fence, walk past huts and into the forest again. Leave by the gate and turn right uphill (not left, the way you came in). Keep on this path through the forest; three types of deer are found here, including red deer, the largest native land mammal in Britain. Walk past fire breaks and follow the green signs with white arrows to the car park. Near the stream in tube culverts, look right where there is a small waterfall. Notice the lichen on the pine trees here, also the mosses and bracken. Follow the path as it curves down to the left. The River Naver comes into view, and you

return to the large gate and the starting point.

POINTS OF INTEREST

Lodgepole Pine
Extensively planted on peat bogs throughout Scotland, lodgepole pine is said to be used for the poles of North American wigwams, hence the name 'lodgepole', and occurs naturally from California to Alaska.

Rosal Village
Rosal Village stands as a monument to the tragic history of the Highland Clearances. It was emptied of its inhabitants in 1814 by landowners, who cleared the villages to make way for Cheviot sheep and increased profits. This system of monoculture, with its bigger and heavier sheep, destroyed the local agriculture and the heather. In its place bracken and rushes took hold of the land. The terrible events of the evictions, by gangs of men burning houses and destroying families, is brought tragically alive in Donald MacLeod's *Gloomy Memories*, a response to the book *Sunny Memories – A Visit to Dunrobin* by Harriet

All-smothering forestry has taken over from the sheep which replaced the people of Strathnaver

Beecher Stowe. It was written as an apologia for the Sutherlands, who were responsible for the most vicious evictions in the Highlands and Islands. Around 15,000 people were cleared from the Sutherland estates. MacLeod himself suffered eviction with his wife. He wrote about the harrowing events, including some around Rosal, near where he was born.

A TREASURE UNDER THREAT
In the 1980s great tracts of the Flow Country were sold off at amazingly low prices (around £15.18 per acre/£37.50 per hectare) for forestation. By 1987 some 79,000 acres (32,000ha) of natural habitat had been ploughed up and drained, causing incalculable ecological damage. It was estimated that 640 pairs of golden plover, 300 pairs of dunlin and 120 pairs of greenshank had their breeding habitat destroyed and there was nowhere else for them to go. This would be tragic enough, even if progress and commerce had been served, but it had been demonstrated that such lands were unsuitable for growing trees. The damage cannot be undone but more is preventable.

THE FLOW COUNTRY Highland

Over half of Caithness and Sutherland is covered by a great swathe of blanket bog – The Flow Country (from the Old Norse, *Flói*, meaning marshy ground). Until very recently it was a landscape which had more or less escaped the attention of human hands. Over a period of some 7,000 years peat accumulated at a very slow rate, often not more than a millimetre per year, reaching a depth of between 16 and 23 feet (5–7m).

The Flow Country is not only unique, but is a natural resource of global importance – a complex mosaic of peat bog and dark, peat-stained pools. Viewed from the ground its almost primeval appearance can't be fully appreciated, but from the air the true beauty, remoteness and expansiveness of the area is quite breathtaking. The barren appearance is deceptive – the area is of immense wildlife importance, with sphagnum moss forming the living skin of the bog, dotted with sundews, sweet scented bog myrtle, heaths and heather.

It is for its birds, though, that it is so very special, particularly the breeding waders, many of which are declining in numbers globally due to the loss of suitable habitats. The Flow Country supports around 70 per cent of the European Community's breeding population of greenshank, together with 20 per cent of the black-throated diver and others such as dunlin and golden plover. In the dimming light of dusk there are few more evocative and thought-provoking experiences than to hear the plaintive 'wheep' of the golden plover or the hauntingly mournful cry of the black-throated diver.

Very few roads traverse this great expanse of land and there are only rare signs of human habitation. Forsinard, lying on the A897, is a good starting point for adventurous walkers, who can also arrive by train. The station buildings house a visitor centre devoted to the ecology of the Flow Country, if a browse arouses your enthusiasm you can accompany the ranger walking in these marvellous boglands.

GOLSPIE AND HELMSDALE Highland Map ref NC8300/ND0315

Golspie and Brora are two delightful little resort towns on the east coast, midway between Inverness and Wick, offering lovely sandy beaches and facilities for sailing, golf and other holiday pastimes. On the wooded hill behind Golspie stands a statue of the 1st Duke of Sutherland. The 2nd Duke was embarrassed here in 1854 when he tried to raise troops to fight in the Crimea – his listeners heard him out before politely reminding him that his family's preference for sheep had depopulated the land, and that nobody could be spared for fighting.

Just up the coast stands the absurdly turreted Dunrobin Castle. Remodelled by the Victorian architect Charles Barry to resemble a French château, it actually dates back to the 13th century, and is the seat of the

Dukes of Sutherland. The castle has served in its time as both a naval hospital and a school. The gardens, modelled on Versailles, are particularly splendid. Beyond Brora, just before the turning at Lothbeg, look out for a stone at the roadside which commemorates the last wolf to be killed in Sutherland.

Set on the coast where the River Helmsdale enters the sea, the little fishing town of Helmsdale has found itself at the centre of several gold rushes over the years. The settlement grew up reluctantly in the 19th century as crofters, cleared from the Strath of Kildonan, were forced to take up herring fishing to survive. Visit the Timespan Heritage Centre which tells this story and much more, from the arrival of the Picts and the Vikings to the discovery of offshore oil.

GOLD FEVER

When alluvial gold was found in the tributaries of the River Helmsdale in 1868, a mini gold rush ensued. While hardly on Klondike scale, the field had yielded £12,000-worth of gold by 1870. You can still pan for gold here. Ask at Strath Ullie Crafts in Helmsdale.

Dunrobin's extraordinary exterior belies a more venerable heart

The Last House Museum draws the tourists to John O'Groats

DUNNET HEAD

The beetling sandstone cliffs at Dunnet Head, 407 feet (124m) high, are a good two miles (3.2km) further north than John O'Groats, and therefore rightly claim to be the northernmost point of mainland Britain. The lighthouse on the clifftop, built by Robert Stevenson, looks out over the turbulent waters of the Pentland Firth, a familiar hazard to sailors, where the Atlantic Ocean meets the North Sea. Windsurfing championships have been held round the corner in the broad, sandy sweep of Dunnet Bay.

JOHN O'GROATS Highland Map ref ND3872

On summer days the tour buses churn into the village at John O'Groats, and churn out again laden with souvenirs. This is not actually the most northerly point on the British mainland at all, but years of publicity – thanks to the eccentrics who walk up here from Land's End to raise money for charity – have drawn the tourists. It's an arduous route, some 870 miles (1,400km) or longer depending on your choice of path, and the cheerful white-painted hotel at the end must have been a very welcome sight for many a weary, foot-sore traveller. The Last House Museum gives an interesting account of the area.

On a clear day you can see northwards beyond the little island of Stroma to Orkney. Dutchman Jan de Groot operated the ferry to South Ronaldsay at the end of the 15th century and gave his name to the settlement – you can find memorials to his family in the old church at Cannisbay, to the west. Her Majesty Queen Elizabeth, The Queen Mother, attends the church here when in residence at her Scottish home, the Castle of Mey (not open). To the east lies Duncansby Head, with a lighthouse and a good walk south along the high cliffs to see the tall stacks of rock just offshore, home to thousands of noisy seabirds, including puffins and cormorants.

There have been various plans over the years to turn John O'Groats into a more serious tourist centre, perhaps along the lines of the controversial complex at Land's End, but these have never quite materialised.

LAIRG AND LOCH SHIN Highland Map ref NC5806
Great expanses of Sutherland are devoid of any human
habitation, the result of the now infamous Clearances in
the late 18th century and first half of the 19th century.
One of the few remaining townships is Lairg, lying at the
southern end of Loch Shin – a vast expanse of fresh
water, 24 miles (38.4km) long and on average a mile
(1.6km) wide.

Stretching away to the north is a pleasant if not
dramatic landscape of mountains, moor, lochans and
streams which occasionally tumble down as waterfalls.
Towards Altnaharra, a tiny village in the middle of
nowhere but a Mecca for salmon anglers, the landscape
is dominated by the towering presence of Ben Kilbrech,
which rises to 3,153 feet (961m).

Lairg has been described as the 'Rome of Sutherland',
the place to which all roads lead, and it is a place of
considerable social and economic importance to the
surrounding area. In August each year there is a one-day
sale of sheep – as many as 250,000 may change hands,
making it easy to believe that every sheep in the region
is there on that day.

There is much to see and admire around Lairg,
including plenty of evidence of earlier habitation in hut
circles, a broch at Sallachy on the southern shore of Loch
Shin and a number of Neolithic stone circles and cairns.
The cairn at The Ord just outside Lairg has been
excavated and is well worth a visit.

The hydro-electric scheme at the southern end of Loch
Shin controls the flow of water in the River Shin, but
salmon are still able to make their way up to the
spawning 'redds'. At the right time of year you can
watch them leaping up the Falls of Shin, a couple of
miles downstream from Lairg, where specially
constructed viewing platforms are provided.

A PLAID TOO FAR

It is an irony of Scottish
history that tartan, that proud
and colourful emblem of a
nation, recognised with
sentimental warmth across
the world, did not reach its
fullest potential until the
commodity of wool became
more widely available. Of
course, as sheep-farming took
over the land, so the
Highlanders were forced off it.

Tartan – the cloth of many
colours woven in formal
patterns of checks and stripes
– emerged as a potent symbol
of clan identity at the end of
the 16th century. By the 18th
century patterns had been
refined into 'setts', but
proscription after the 1745
uprising resulted in the
destruction of many records.
Today the tartan industry
thrives on a spirit of Scots
kinship, with new patterns
and colourways to suit
modern fashion, and its
application to every Scottish
souvenir you could imagine.

*The small township of Lairg
is famous for its annual
sheep sales*

PUFFINS
Of all the seabirds familiar
around the northern coast of
Scotland, the rotund puffin is
one of the favourites. With
their big, brightly coloured
bills and red feet, puffins are
easily recognised, and while
the biggest breeding colony is
on inaccessible St Kilda, their
burrows are also to be found
at many other points around
the coast in cliffs and on
grassy slopes. July is probably
the best month to observe
these comical little birds, but
you may see them any time
between March and August.

SCOURIE Highland Map ref NC1544

The village of Scourie lies on the shores of Edrachillis
Bay, and thanks to the warm air of the Gulf Stream this
is the northernmost point in Britain where Atlantic palm
trees will grow – you can see them growing in the
gardens of Scourie House. This was the home of General
Hugh Mackay, born here in 1640, who was a Covenanter
and soldier, rising to become commander-in-chief in the
Highlands. Linked with events at Killiecrankie and
Cromdale, Mackay is credited with the invention of the
offset bayonet.

Scourie is a popular centre for walkers and anglers, and
especially with birdwatchers who come in early summer
to visit the nature reserve on nearby Handa Island.
Handa once supported as many as seven families, ruled
by their own 'queen' – traditionally the oldest widow.
The last islanders were driven away in the 1840s when
the potato harvests failed, and today the birds reign
supreme on the cliffs – thousands of wheeling gulls,
guillemots, kittiwakes, puffins and razorbills. In the care
of the Scottish Wildlife Trust, Handa can be reached by
boat from just up the coast at Tarbet.

East of Scourie, the River Laxford, crossed by the A838
at Laxford Bridge, is noted for its salmon, and there are
numerous lochans to explore in this wild landscape. The
hills here are rugged lumps of Torridon sandstone
– inland, Foinaven 2,979 feet (908m) and Arkle 2,579
feet (786m) gave their names to famous racehorses.
Continue north up the A838 and turn off for
Kinlochbervie to see a busy fishing port in action. This
road ends at Shegra, but you can walk on to enjoy the
delights of beautiful, secluded Sandwood Bay.

THURSO Highland Map ref ND1168

After travelling across the vast empty expanse of Sutherland it is somehow surprising to arrive at such a thriving little town on the north coast. The Vikings were probably the first to spot the potential of this location, where a good salmon river pours through a long, narrow harbour and into the bay. Orkney can be glimpsed across the stormy waters of the Pentland Firth, and is reached via the ferries which leave from nearby Scrabster.

Thurso developed not so much as a fishing port, but rather a bustling centre for trade, especially with Scandinavia. Meat, fish and notably grain from Caithness were exported with such success that the town's system of weights was adopted as the standard for Scotland. Local flagstones were shipped around the world. With the fall in trade the town might have died, but fortunes revived with the building of the Dounreay nuclear plant, which is still a key employer, though most of the 1,200 workforce are focussed on decommissioning the site. The visitor centre is well worth a visit.

Thurso's prosperous history is reflected in its wide main streets and pleasant squares. Look out for royal coats of arms over various doorways – Her Majesty Queen Elizabeth, The Queen Mother, shops here. It is also worth visiting the heritage museum in the Town Hall. The curiously dignified shell of St Peter's Church dates from the 12th century. Later restored, it was finally abandoned in the 19th century and now stands open to the skies. The statue of Sir John Sinclair (1745–1835) commemorates the great agriculturalist, who pioneered many new ideas in northern Scotland. There is a portrait of him, by Raeburn, in the Scottish National Portrait Gallery in Edinburgh, which shows a tall man dressed determinedly in tartan 'trews' – he apparently considered them more authentic and practical than the kilt.

'THE FOUNDER'

William Smith was born in Pennyland House, on the western outskirts of Thurso, in 1854, the son of a former dragoons officer. Brought up in Glasgow, from a young age he became an active member of the Free College Church and of the Lanarkshire Volunteers. Embracing the Victorian spirit of 'muscular Christianity', he founded the Boys' Brigade in 1883 for 'the advancement of Christ's Kingdom among Boys', an organisation which gave predominantly urban boys a sense of discipline, purpose and Christian brotherhood. More regimental than the Boy Scouts, which started later, it is still going strong today.

The empty shell of old St Peter's lies near the centre of Thurso

Fishing boats at rest in the harbour at Wick

FLAGSTONES
Underlying much of Caithness is a grey, thinly bedded, carbonate-rich siltstone. This has been widely exploited in the area, the thin layers of stone cut and polished as flagstones, which can be seen everywhere as paving, roofing and even forming walls. Flagstones quarried at Castleton were exported from Thurso during the 19th century, and appear all over the world, from London's Euston Station to Melbourne, Australia. The industry was finally elbowed out by the more convenient pre-cast concrete, but some flagstones are still quarried here.

WICK Highland Map ref ND3650
Traditionally locked into rivalry with Thurso, the town takes its name from the Norse word for a bay, *vik*, and the oldest part lies to the north of the river. To the south, Pultneytown was laid out by Thomas Telford for the British Fisheries Society in the early 19th century. With its substantial harbour, the timing was just right to take advantage of the herring glut. The town prospered, its numbers swelled by migrant workers from western Scotland and Ireland. The curing yard and old photographs at the heritage centre recall Wick's heyday, when the harbour bristled with fishing boats.

Today's invaders are probably in search of bargains at the Caithness Glass factory shop, but older times brought the Vikings, and the imposing castle of Old Wick dates from those violent days. More ruined forts litter the northward coast. Castles Girnigoe and Sinclair stand side by side on Noss Head; an over-eager Sinclair heir was incarcerated in the former for seven horrible years before apparently dying of starvation and 'vermin'. A couple of miles west is Ackergill Tower, remodelled in the 19th century. At the top of Sinclairs Bay, near the remains of two Iron-Age brochs, 16th-century Keiss Castle stands on the precipitous cliff edge. A more comfortable Baronial-style replacement was built inland in the 19th century.

Caithness and Sutherland

Leisure Information

Places of Interest

Shopping

The Performing Arts

Sports, Activities and the Outdoors

Annual Events and Customs

Checklist

Leisure Information

TOURIST INFORMATION CENTRES

Bettyhill
Clachan (Seasonal). Tel: 01641 521342.
Dornoch
The Square.
Tel: 01862 810400.
Durness
Sango. Tel: 01971 511259.
John O'Groats
County Road (Seasonal).
Tel: 01955 611373.
Lairg
(Seasonal.) Tel: 01549 402160.
Lochinver
Main Street (Seasonal).
Tel: 01571 844330.
Thurso
Riverside (Seasonal). Tel: 01847 892371.
Wick
Whitechapel Road. Tel: 01955 602596.

OTHER INFORMATION

Ferries
Caledonian MacBrayne Ferries
Ferry Terminal, Gourock.
Tel: 01475 650100. For the
Hebrides via the Firth of Clyde,
or the many ports on the west
coast with sailings to 23 islands.

Two excellent value 'rover'
tickets are offered.
P & O Scottish Ferries
Jamiesons Quay, Aberdeen.
Tel: 01224 572615. Daily
sailings to Orkney from Scrabster
(Thurso). Sailings from Orkney
(Stromness) to Shetland
(Lerwick). Also sailings from
Aberdeen.
Forest Enterprise
Forestry Commision, 231
Corstorphine Road, Edinburgh.
Tel: 0131 334 0303.
**Highlands of Scotland
Tourist Board**
www.host.co.uk
Historic Scotland
Longmore House, Salisbury
Place, Edinburgh. Tel: 0131 668
8800.
Met Office
www.meto.gov.uk
National Trust for Scotland
28 Charlotte Square, Edinburgh.
Tel: 0131 243 9300.
www.nts.org.uk
RSPB
Dunedin House, 25 Ravelston
Terrace, Edinburgh. Tel: 0131
311 6500. www.rspb.com
Scottish Tourist Board
23 Ravelston Terrace,
Edinburgh. Tel: 0131 332 2433.
www.visitscotland.com

Scottish Wildlife Trust
Cramond House, Cramond
Glebe Road. Edinburgh. Tel:
0131 312 7765.
www.swt.org.uk
Weather
Weathercall for northwest
Scotland. Tel: 09068 232795.

ORDNANCE SURVEY MAPS

Landranger 1:50,000 sheets
9, 10, 11, 12, 15, 16, 17, 20,
21.

Places of Interest

There will be an admission
charge at the following places of
interest unless otherwise stated.
Ardvreck Castle
On the A837 by Loch Assynt.
Built in 1490, now a ruin and
unsafe. Information leaflet from
Lochinver Tourist Information
Centre. Always open. Free.
Cape Wrath
Twelve miles (19.2km) northwest of Durness. The most
northerly point of Scotland's
north-west seaboard. Passenger
ferry (summer only) connects
with minibus service to the
Cape. Ferry: Tel: 01971 511376.
Mini bus: Tel: 01971 511287/
511343.

Castles Girnigoe and Sinclair
Noss Head. 3 miles (4.8km)
north of Wick. Ruined clifftop
castles. Always open. Free.

**Clan Gunn Heritage Centre
and Museum**
Latheron, Helmsdale. 16 miles
(25.7km) southwest of Wick.
Tel: 01593 721325. Open
Jun–Sep, most days.

Dounreay Exhibition Centre
On the A836 west of Thurso.
Tel: 01847 802714.
Open mid-May to Oct.
Free.

Dunbeath Heritage Centre
Old School, Dunbeath.
Tel: 01593 731233. Open
Easter–Oct, daily.

**Dunrobin Castle and
Gardens**
One mile (1.6km) northeast of
Golspie on A9. Tel: 01408
633177. Open Apr to mid-Oct,
daily.

Flagstone Trail
Castlehill, Castleton, A836, 4
miles (6.4km) east of Thurso.
Original source of flagstones
exported worldwide. Outside
trail showing quarrying, stone-
dressing and harbour from

which the flagstones were
exported. Free.

Flow Country Visitor Centre
Forsinard.
Open May–Sep daily.

Grey Cairns of Camister
Five miles (8km) north of
Lybster, Wick.
Tel: 0131 668 8800. Megalithic
cairns. Near by are the Clyth
stone rows and Achavannich
Stone Circle. Always open.
Free.

Laidhay Croft Museum
On the A9 just north of
Dunbeath. Tel: 01593 731244.
Open Easter to mid-Oct, daily.

Northlands Viking Centre
On the A99, Auckengill. Tel:
01847 805518. Traces the Norse
settlement of Caithness.

Orcadian Stone Company
Main Street, Golspie. Tel: 01408
633483. Exhibition of local
geology; also fine mineral
specimens from all over the
world. Charge for museum.
Open all year most days.

Smoo Cave
Durness. Contact Durness
Tourist Information Centre.
Tel: 01971 511259. Vast

limestone caves. Open all
reasonable times. Free.

Strathnaver Museum
Bettyhill. Tel: 01641 521418.
Open Apr–Oct, Mon–Sat.

Strath Ullie Crafts
The Harbour, Helmsdale.
Tel: 01431 821402. Panning
for gold in Kildonan Burn,
9 miles (14.4km) from
Helmsdale. The shop hires out
gold-panning equipment, and
gives advice on the best places
to try your luck and how to go
about it. Open all year most
days.

Thurso Heritage Museum
Town Hall, High Street, Thurso.
Open Jun–Sep, most days.

Timespan Heritage Centre
Dunrobin Street, Helmsdale.
Tel: 01431 821327. Open
Easter–Oct, daily.

Wick Heritage Centre
20 Bank Row, Wick. Tel: 01955
605393. Open Jun–Sep, most
days.

*The magnificent curving
sweep of Dunnet Bay has
proved popular with wind-
surfers*

SPECIAL INTEREST FOR CHILDREN

The following places may be of interest to visitors with children. Unless otherwise stated there will be an admission charge.

Fossil Visitor Centre
Village Hall, Spittal. On the A9 south of Thurso. Tel: 01847 841266. Open Jun–Sep, certain days.

Highland and Rare Breeds Farm
Elphin, on the A835 14 miles (22.5km) north of Ullapool. Tel: 01854 666204. Open mid-May to Aug, daily.

Kingspark Llama Farm
Berriedale, northeast of Helmsdale. Tel: 01593 751202. Open all year, daily.

Shopping

LOCAL SPECIALITIES

Crafts
Dornoch Craft Centre, Town Jail, Dornoch. Tel: 01862 810555. Tartan weaving and exhibitions.

Distillery
Clynelish Distillery, on the northern outskirts of Brora. Tel: 01408 623000. Open all year weekdays only.

Glass
Caithness Glass Factory and Visitor Centre, Airport Industrial Estate, Wick. Tel: 01955 602286. Viewing gallery and exhibition. Free.

The Performing Arts

Lyth Arts Centre
Between Wick and John O'Groats. Tel: 01955 641270. Art exhibitions and touring theatre and music performances. See local press or call for details.

Sports, Activities and the Outdoors

ANGLING

Fly
Dornoch Lochans Fishery. Tel: 01862 810600. For further information on angling, enquire at local Tourist Information Centres.

BOAT TRIPS

Enard Bay
Badnaban Cruises. South of Lochinver. Tel: 01571 844358. Small boats to seal and bird colonies in Enard Bay.

Loch Glencoul
Statesman Cruises. A894 over Locha Chairn Bhain. Kylesku Bridge. Tel: 01571 844446. Boat cruises up Loch Glencoul to Eas Coul Aulin waterfall.

Smoo Cave
Cape Sea Tours, boat trip to Smoo Cave, and to see local wildlife. Contact Durness Tourist Information Centre. Tel: 01971 511365.

COUNTRY PARKS, FORESTS AND NATURE RESERVES

Handa Island Nature Reserve
Three miles (4.8km) northwest of Scourie. Seabird sanctuary with guided walks. Small open ferry from Tarbet, 4 miles (6.4km) north of Scourie, for boat trips.

GOLF COURSES

Bonar Bridge
Bonar Bridge Golf Club. Tel: 01863 766750 (secretary).

Brora
Brora Golf Club, Golf Road. Tel: 01408 621417.

Dornoch
Royal Dornoch Golf Club, Golf Road. Tel: 01862 810219.

Durness
Durness Golf Club. A mile (1.6km) west of Durness. Tel: 01971 511364.

Golspie
Golspie Golf Club, Ferry Road. Off A9 half a mile (0.8km) south of Golspie. Tel: 01408 633266.

Lybster
Lybster Golf Club, Main Street. (No telephone number.)

Reay
Reay Golf Club. Tel: 01847 811288.

Thurso
Thurso Golf Club. Two miles (3.2km) west of Thurso. Tel: 01847 892575 (secretary).

Wick
Wick Golf Club. Signposted on the A9 north of Wick. Tel: 01955 602726.

HORSE-RIDING

Thurso
Achalone Activities, Halkirk, Caithness. On the B874, 8 miles (12.8km) from Thurso. Tel: 01847 831326.

Annual Events and Customs

Thurso
Caithness Highland Gathering and Games, early July.

The checklists give details of just some of the facilities within the area covered by this guide. Further information can be obtained from Tourist Information Centres

The Northern Isles
ORKNEY ISLANDS

The 90 or more islands and skerries of the Orkney Islands are like a handful of emeralds cast on the waters of the North Atlantic, their gentle, green, undulating landscape in sharp contrast to the rugged scenery of the north mainland of Scotland. There is a sensation of space, with never-ending skies and great expanses of ocean. Time has not stood still, but there is a timelessness here which is difficult to describe but impossible to ignore. Modern times arrived with the North Sea oil industry, but reminders of a long history are all around, from evocative standing stones and other great prehistoric monuments, through great buildings such as Kirkwall Cathedral, to the Italian Chapel and the silent sentinels of World War II gun emplacements.

THE BA' GAME

This twice annual event, held at Christmas and New Year, probably originated in rivalry between the youths of two parts of the town when Kirkwall was granted the Scottish Royal Charter in 1486. In its present form, the game has been played since around 1850. The 'Uppies' play the 'Doonies', with team members' allegiance decided by birthplace – 'up or doon the gate'. Up to 200 'players' may be involved – the Doonies have to get the ba' to the sea (normally Kirkwall harbour); the Uppies' goal is the junction of Main Street and New Scapa Road. At the end of the game an individual winner is named by popular acclaim, and the title is regarded as a great honour.

KIRKWALL Map ref HY4411

The first reference to Kirkwall is as *Kirkjuvagr*, Old Norse for Church Bay, which appears under the date 1046 in the great Norse saga *The Orkneyinga Saga*. Kirkwall never gained prominence as a great sea port, but nevertheless became an important settlement which grew rapidly with the building of the cathedral. Much remains of the old town which developed between the 16th and 18th centuries, with narrow winding streets and lanes and compact houses, often with their gable ends on to the street. Above all this, St Magnus' Cathedral dominates the town and it is also the centrepiece of a rich collection of fine architecture dating from the 12th to 17th centuries.

St Magnus' Cathedral is one of only two intact pre-Reformation cathedrals in Scotland. Built of local red and yellow sandstone, it is a building of magnificent robustness which from the outside gives no indication of the wonderful feeling of space and tranquillity inside. Earl Rognvald started the building in 1137; he was the nephew of Earl Magnus, who had been murdered by his own cousin, Earl Haakon, some 20 years earlier and whose bones are contained within the massive north choir pillar. The cathedral was not completed, however, until sometime in the 15th century.

Clustered around the cathedral are the ruins of the Bishop's Palace, dating from between the 12th and 16th centuries, and the Earl's Palace (1606), which has been described as the most mature and accomplished piece of Renaissance architecture left in Scotland. The main entrance, the oriel windows and the great fireplace in the hall are particularly outstanding features. Tankerness House (1580), now a museum, was originally occupied by the clergy of the cathedral and later acquired and added to by the Baikies of Tankerness, wealthy merchants of that time.

MAES HOWE   Map ref HY3313

Maes Howe stands in a field at the south end of the Loch of Harray, near to the A965, the main road between Stromness and Finstown. The massive chambered cairn, dating from around 2800 BC is one of the great treasures of the art of the prehistoric European mason. The mound itself is almost 115 feet (35m) in diameter and 23 feet (7m) high, surrounded by a low bank and ditch. The inner chamber is nearly 15 feet (4.5m) square, lined by beautifully fitting stone slabs with a corbelled roof, with three side chambers built into the walls. You enter through a passage over 47 feet (14.5m) long and nearly 5 feet (1.4m) high, lined by huge stone slabs, the largest of which is estimated to weigh more than three tonnes. The interior of the tomb is awesome, and we can only wonder at the forces and beliefs that drove these people to undertake a project of this scale with such skill and dedication.

Inevitably the chambered cairn was broken into and the contents plundered many centuries ago, but the structure has survived more or less intact. The loss of the contents can never be fully compensated for, but the Norsemen who broke in and sought shelter from a great storm here have left a magnificent legacy of Runic inscriptions, together with other stone carvings, including a walrus, a serpent knot and a dragon.

STANDING STONES

There are a great many standing stones in the Orkney Islands, mostly monoliths or pairs, but including the two great circles of the Ring of Brodgar and the Stones of Stenness. Of all the stone monuments in Orkney, the Ring of Brodgar is the most evocative. Originally a perfect circle of 60 stones, only 27 are still standing. Such construction by Neolithic people represents a massive commitment. Experts have estimated that the excavation of the ditch around the Ring of Brodgar would have taken some 80,000 man-hours to dig, even before the stones themselves were cut, transported and erected. The wonder of these massive monuments is all the greater for the mystery which still surrounds their true purpose. The global importance of Orkney's Neolithic sites was recognised when they were added to the UNESCO list of World Heritage Sites.

The grassy mound of Maes Howe conceals an ancient burial chamber

Midhowe broch stands exposed on a promontory

ISLAND WILDLIFE

The northern islands are a wildlife paradise. The cliffs, maritime heaths, moorlands, freshwater lochs, beaches and sea are home to a range of birds. The elusive corncrake can still be heard, if not seen, on Papa Westray, and many other birds visit in the summer to breed, including red-throated divers, Arctic terns, Arctic skuas, great skuas, fulmars and kittiwakes, along with various auks. The maritime heath supports a rich flora, including heath spotted orchid, spring squill with its profusion of delicate sky blue flowers, and both the primrose and Scottish primrose, *Primula scotica*. The seashores around the islands range from exposed rocky headlands to sheltered sandy bays, and support a wide range of wildlife. Common and grey seals are to be seen, and otters also frequent the shore, but are more wary of human company and more difficult to see.

ROUSAY AND OTHER ISLANDS

The 15 main northern islands of Orkney have names to conjure with – Eynhallow (Holy Isle), Eday (Isthmus Isle), Wyre (Spearhead Isle) and Sanday (Sandy Isle). Each has a unique character and a particular contribution to make to the history and culture of the Orcadians, such as the collecting of cast kelp, or 'tangle', or the North Ronaldsay breed of sheep which have evolved to graze the seaweed on the shore and cannot digest grass.

All the islands are worth visiting, either by ferry or by air (flights include the shortest scheduled air route in the world, taking less than 2 minutes for the 1½-mile/2.4km hop between Westray and Papa Westray). Many of the island air strips are simply fields, making the most exciting part of the flight the avoiding of cow pats on landing and take-off!

Rousay, across Eynhallow Sound from the mainland of Orkney, is one of the largest of this group. Its two high points are Blotchnie Fiold (820 feet/250m) and Kierfa (771 feet/235m), and the climb is rewarded by panoramic views of the islands. Rousay has been inhabited for at least 5,000 years and all around are chambered cairns, brochs, Viking sites and medieval ruins. On an island littered with relics, Midhowe Cairn and Midhowe Broch, overlooking Eynhallow Sound, stand out. Midhowe Cairn, from the 3rd millennium BC, is one of the finest examples of a chambered cairn so far discovered. The remains of 25 people were unearthed during the excavations, including nine complete skeletons. The broch, occupied between 200 BC and AD 200, is built on a promontory, with outer defences on the landward side. Artefacts found here included some of Roman origin, bone and stone spindle whorls and evidence of both iron and bronze workings.

SCAPA FLOW AND HOY

The sheltered waters of Scapa Flow were an important naval anchorage in the two World Wars, and are famous for the sinking of HMS *Royal Oak* by the German submarine *U47* in 1939. This prompted the construction of the Churchill Barriers – a great causeway littered with blocks of concrete, linking Mainland to the islands of Lamb Holm, Glimps Holm, Burray and South Ronaldsay, cutting off access by sea from the east. Italian prisoners of war worked on the Barriers and created their own extraordinary monument – the Italian Chapel on Lamb Holm, converted from two Nissen huts. The craftsmanship and faith which have so evidently gone into the chapel's decoration leave you with a sense of deep admiration for human ingenuity.

Drive across the Barriers, down the eastern chain of islands, and you will find that they typify the lush farmland of Orkney. Unlike the rest of Orkney, however, there is a dearth of archaeological relics. A notable exception is the chambered cairn on South Ronaldsay, known as the 'Tomb of the Eagles'. Around 340 people were buried here over a period of some 800 years up to 2200 BC, but the name comes from the skeletons of sea eagles also found there.

Hoy (Old Norse *Ha-ey*, meaning 'high land') forms the southwest boundary to Scapa Flow, and of all the Orkney Islands this is most like the Highlands of Scotland, with heather moor supporting a range of sub-Arctic and alpine plants together with a wide variety of birds. There are marvellous opportunities for vigorous walks, and those who make it to the top of Ward Hill (1,555 feet/477m) or Cuilags (1420 feet/433m) will be rewarded with fabulous views of the Flow and the other islands. In the valley between Ward Hill and the Dwarfie Hammars lies the Dwarfie Stane, a unique chambered cairn, hollowed out of a slab of sandstone using only stone implements.

THE GERMAN FLEET

Scapa Flow was home to the Royal Navy in both World Wars, but even their presence could not rival the sight of the German High Seas Fleet which was escorted to Scapa Flow in 1919 after the surrender of Germany at the end of World War I – 74 vessels in all, including battleships, battle cruisers and destroyers.

On 21 June 1919 the entire fleet was scuttled by their skeleton German crews on receipt of the order 'paragraph eleven' from Admiral Reuters. Many vessels have since been salvaged, but 12 remain on the sea bed of Scapa Flow, including the battleships *Kronprinz Wilhelm*, *Markgraf* and *König*. These vessels, although in relatively deep water, are now a great attraction for visiting scuba divers.

The steep purple hills of Hoy are seen clearly from the mainland

A glimpse of prehistoric life is caught in the ancient dwellings of Skara Brae

THE PEOPLES OF ORKNEY

Little is known about the first settlers of Orkney, around 6,000 years ago, but burial sites around the islands offer a tantalising clue to a culture that honoured their dead. The Picts arrived in around 700 BC, and even less is known about them, although they too have left monuments in the form of brochs. Christianity arrived in the 5th century and soon after that came the golden age of the Vikings, whose legacy was the most lasting. Many island place-names are derived from Old Norse, and architectural feats include St Magnus' Cathedral and the Brough of Birsay settlements. It wasn't until the 13th century that the Orkney Islands became a part of Scotland – as part of the dowry of Margaret of Denmark on her marriage to James III of Scotland.

SKARA BRAE Map ref HY2318

The remains of the Neolithic settlement of Skara Brae are now almost at the high water mark and, if it wasn't for the protection of a sea wall, they would be seriously threatened by erosion. When it was inhabited, between 3100 BC and 2500 BC, the village was separated from the sea by sand dunes and a freshwater loch. The dunes eventually swallowed up and covered the site until 1850, when a great storm swept away enough of the sand to show the presence of stone structures. Further excavation revealed this to be a priceless piece of Orcadian archaeological heritage, giving a remarkable glimpse of domestic life in earlier centuries.

Over the 600 years that the settlement was inhabited, rebuilding and modification took place, but what you see today are six remarkably similar rectangular houses linked together by narrow winding passages, all embedded in a surrounding midden (now tastefully grassed over). Each house has a central hearth, small cells or cupboards recessed into the walls, slab-built beds, a stone dresser, and clay-lined stone boxes sunk into the floor. The entrances are small, and could be barred and secured from the inside. The roofs would have been of turf and animal skin, laid over driftwood and whalebone. Broken pottery, chert tools and jewellery found here suggest that there would have been as many as 50 people living at Skara Brae at any one time. We can only wonder about the lives those early settlers may have led – on a fine summer's day it seems almost idyllic, but in midwinter no-one would envy the rigours they must have endured.

STROMNESS   Map ref HY2508

The sea has always been the life blood of Stromness, situated on the safe and sheltered shores of Hamnavoe, and it remains so to this day – the ferry, the *St Ola*, runs between here and Scrabster on the Scottish mainland. The over-riding importance of the sea to the early residents of Stromness is apparent in that most of the earliest houses are at the sea edge, gable end on, and each has its own pier or slipway. You get a good impression of this from the windows of the splendid Pier Arts Centre. If this is the first impression of most visitors, the second is of the main street through Stromness – a narrow, winding, paved and cobbled road.

Before the advent of regular Atlantic voyages, Stromness was little more than a hamlet – there were just 21 houses and shops here in 1792. That was before the Arctic whaling industry and trade with Canada (particularly the Hudson Bay Company) sparked its growth to over 500 homes by 1841. The full story is told in the excellent Stromness Museum.

Visiting vessels brought prosperity to Stromness, their last stop before Greenland or America (the great explorers Captain Cook and Sir James Franklin were among them). They needed large quantities of provisions for their voyages, including fresh water from Login's Well, which can still be seen. Sometimes the vessels also took on crew, and for a time the narrow streets provided ideal hunting grounds for the Royal Navy press gangs. Shipping activity reached its peak with the herring boom of the late 19th and early 20th centuries – at its peak there could be over 400 boats in and around Hamnavoe – but by 1907 it was all over, the stocks of herring exhausted by over fishing. The same thing, of course, is still happening in the world today – different fish, but the same greed and short-sightedness.

ORKNEY WHISKY

Until the 1920s Orkney had three distilleries, but the Old Orkney distillery in Stromness fell victim to the Temperance Movement which gained support in the town which was dry between 1920 and 1947. This left Highland Park Distillery in Kirkwall, and Scapa, across Scapa Bay. Scapa, established in 1885, produced a smoky, salty dram, aged in Bourbon flasks, but the plant was mothballed in 1994 and has not produced since. Highland Park on Holm Road in Kirkwall, established in 1825, just two years after distilling was legalised. It is one of the few distilleries which still malts its own barley, feeding the four stills which produce an aristocratic 12-year-old whisky with a unique silky flavour. There is an excellent reception centre and conducted tours are available.

Older houses crowd the inner harbour at Stromness

FAIR ISLE SHIPWRECKS
On average, Fair Isle endures 64 days a year of winds exceeding 34 knots, and gusts of 64 knots (hurricane force) are not uncommon. Combine this with the vagaries of the currents and the fog which can roll in to envelop the island and you have a sure recipe for shipwrecks. Little is known of those which occurred before the 19th century – with the notable exception of the *El Gran Grifon*, a troop ship of the Spanish Armada which foundered there in 1588. In 1868 a German migrant ship, the *Lessing*, was wrecked, but the courage and seamanship of the islanders saved all 465 people, who were taken off the stricken vessel in the local long, narrow rowing boats known as yoles. Lighthouses at each end of the island were commissioned in 1892, but still the wrecks continue.

FAIR ISLE AND FOULA

Between them, Fair Isle (Old Norse *Fridarey* – 'truce island') and Foula (Old Norse for 'island of birds') are two of Britain's loveliest and remotest inhabited islands and yet few people have been privileged to visit them, despite links by both air and sea between Shetland and Fair Isle. Fair Isle lies almost equidistant between Orkney and Shetland, some 25 miles (40.2km) to the south of Sumburgh Head – to many people just a dot in the ocean which deserves a mention on the shipping forecasts. Foula lies 14 miles (22.5km) to the west of Shetland, its precipitous sandstone cliffs rising to towering heights of 1,220 feet (372m).

FAIR ISLE

There are a number of good reasons for visiting Fair Isle, not least the prehistoric remains near Funniquoy Hill and Vaasetter, and the remains of an Iron-Age fort at Landberg. The Haa House, dating from around the 18th century, was where Sir Walter Scott stayed when he visited the island in 1814. Archaeological records show that the island has been inhabited since before 1000 BC. It has a ruggedly beautiful coastline of steep cliffs rising to around 590 feet (180m) at their highest, interspersed with stacks, arches and caves sculpted by the continuous erosion by the unrelenting weather and waves. The sea surrounding Fair Isle, known as The Roost, is infamous for the roughness of its troubled waters at the meeting of the contrary currents of the Atlantic Ocean and the North Sea.

Most of today's human visitors come to admire the spectacular scenery and birdlife for which Fair Isle is famous. It was in recognition of the great importance of Fair Isle, both as a stop-over for migrating birds and as a breeding site, that George Waterston established what is now an internationally renowned bird observatory. By the end of 2001, over 358 species of bird had been recorded, and of those only 35 were resident or regular summer breeding species. Fair Isle can boast no fewer than 17 'new for Britain' records and a further 15 'new for Scotland' ones.

The isolated island of Fair Isle is owned by the National Trust for Scotland

In the spring the birds are all in their finest breeding plumage and you are treated to vivid displays such as the bluethroats, with their startling blue bibs with a scarlet spot. Autumn is the time to see the rare and unusual visitors, and each year the list of species is different. The majestic sea cliffs are also ideal for a whole range of breeding seabirds. Of the 24 species which regularly breed in Britain, 17 occur on Fair Isle, amounting in total to around 100,000 pairs. At the height of the breeding season the cliffs and sky are a blizzard of birds – various auks, Arctic and great skuas, terns, gannets, common gulls and storm petrels to name but a few. It is a spectacle which has to be seen (and heard) to be believed.

FOULA

As the summer sun sinks slowly in the western sky, framing the distinctive, ragged outline of Foula in a fiery backdrop of reds and golds, it creates a truly memorable image. Life on Foula has always been a remote and isolated existence and, despite the improved ferry service to mainland Shetland and an air service, the people of Foula still live in the past – literally. It is one of the few places left in Europe, if not the world, to observe the old Julian Calendar, which means that Christmas Day is celebrated on what is 6 January to the rest of us, and New Year's Day falls on 13 January!

Crofting, fishing, spinning and weaving provide the main source of income for the islanders, although tourism is increasing, particularly attracting those who crave peace and solitude. Visitors come here both to appreciate the beauty of the land and seascapes and to study the wildlife. There are superb opportunities to observe seabirds – 18 species breed here, including puffins, guillemots, razorbills, fulmars, storm petrels and Leach's petrels, together with the largest and densest colony of great skua anywhere in the world.

Sunset over Foula, from Eshaness

FOULA DAYS
The Julian Calendar was a solar rather than lunar dating system, established by Julius Caesar on the advice of the Alexandrian astronomer, Sosigenes. The year was 365¼ days long, divided into 12 months, each with either 30 or 31 days, except February which had 28 days or 29 days in leap years. It sounds familiar, but Sosigenes had made a miscalculation, overestimating the length of the year by 11 minutes 14 seconds!

By the mid-16th century the seasons had shifted by about 10 days. Pope Gregory III ordered a reform of the calendar in 1582, which advanced the date by 10 days. The only difference between the calendars is that no century year is a leap year unless exactly divisible by 400. Further fine tuning states that any year evenly divisible by 4,000 should not be a leap year, and this ensures that the Gregorian Calendar remains accurate to 1 day in 20,000 years.

THE NORTHERN LIGHTS
Undoubtedly the greatest light-show on earth, the Northern Lights (*Aurora Borealis*) are a not infrequent sight in Shetland on clear winter nights, although they are predominantly a phenomenon of the high latitudes. Great shimmering lights ranging in colour from pure violet white through the whole spectrum to red can be seen on occasions, and no two shows are the same. They are the product of solar flares which send charged particles hurtling through space, only to discharge their energy as light in the upper atmosphere. They must have seemed a very strange and mysterious spectacle to the ancient peoples living on the islands, and may well have been the source of the mythological Valkyries of Norse legend.

SHETLAND

The Shetland Islands are the most northerly part of the UK – early Roman writers, referring to *Ultima Thule*, 'the end of the world', almost certainly meant Shetland. The islands lie almost equidistant from Aberdeen, Tórshavn in the Faroes and Bergen in Norway; Lerwick, the capital, is nearer to the Arctic Circle than to London. The archipelago of more than 100 islands, of which only around 20 are inhabited, is actually the tops of a range of hills that were drowned by the rise in sea level at the end of the last Ice Age. This is a distinctive and invigorating landscape of low-lying hills, peat-covered moors and water – a place where it is difficult, if not impossible, to ignore the forces of nature.

FETLAR

Fetlar is unusual amongst the Shetland Islands in being particularly fertile, as indicated by its Old Norse name meaning 'fat land'. It has a beautiful scenic coastline with a number of archaeological reminders of the past, from the Neolithic chambered cairn at Vord Hill to the Giant's Grave at Aith – an obscure Norse burial site. The wildlife is remarkable and a large part of the island is an RSPB nature reserve. Fetlar gained recognition for the snowy owls which returned and bred there for a few years between 1967 and 1975. It is also important for its red-throated divers, beautiful, elegant birds which favour only the remotest places for nesting. Breeding auks and wintering wildfowl, together with seals and otters are just some of the highlights of the island's wildlife.

JARLSHOF AND ST NINIAN'S ISLE Map ref HU4009

In much the same way as a great storm exposed the settlement of Skara Brae, so it was in 1905 that the ancient archaeological remains at Jarlshof at the southern end of Shetland were discovered. The site is dominated by the towering ruin of the 17th-century

The ruins of a 17th-century house watch over the much older remains of Jarlshof

Laird's House, which overlies a prehistoric broch. This house was originally known as Sumburgh, until Sir Walter Scott renamed it 'Jarlshof' in his novel *The Pirate*. The name has stuck, and is now taken to refer to the whole site.

Jarlshof embraces Neolithic, Bronze-Age, Iron-Age, Pictish, Norse and medieval remains. A farm from the Viking period is particularly well preserved. The earliest Norse structure is the 9th-century Hall House, measuring nearly 69 feet (21m) in length, which had a central hearth, with low benches down each side and timber posts to help support the roof. Various extensions and modifications were made to this original design over the next four centuries. The succeeding medieval farm, built probably in the first part of the 14th century and inhabited until the end of the 15th, is a rare early example of a design of farm which was still being built in the 18th and 19th centuries. The dwelling house and byre were built parallel and close together, with a kiln for drying corn in the corner of the byre. As a record of human habitation in Shetland through the ages, Jarlshof is a supreme example.

Just up the west coast, lovely St Ninian's Isle is connected to the mainland by a tongue of white sand, or tombolo, which affords access for most of the time, except at exceptionally high tides. A small, beautiful, uninhabited island, this was where St Ninian, the first Christian missionary to travel to Shetland, made his base, although his main monastery was at Whithorn in Dumfries and Galloway. The ruins of a medieval church, built in the 12th and 13th centuries on the site of a much earlier church, are still there. In 1958 a trove of Pictish silver was found under a stone slab beneath the nave, consisting of 28 objects, all beautifully worked and decorated (these are displayed in Edinburgh).

St Ninian's emerald island is linked to the mainland by a sand bar, or tombolo

THE PICTS

The Picts 'enter' into history in AD 279 when the Roman poet Eumenius described the inhabitants of Northern Britain by that name, which means 'the painted ones'. These people can be considered as the true aboriginals of Scotland and are surrounded by many unanswered and unanswerable questions. What was their real name? What is the meaning of the series of symbols they have left as engravings? Whatever else, they were certainly talented craftsmen, able to work fine patterns into their silver jewellery and stone monuments. But what of the Pictish symbol stones? Are they memorials to the dead? Were they notices proclaiming territorial rights? Did they record allegiances formed by marriages? The final enigma, however, is what happened to the Picts? In the middle of the 9th century they disappeared from recorded history.

UP HELLY AA

The annual fire festival known as Up Helly Aa is held in Lerwick at the end of January. Although it is the creation of Victorian romanticism, it has important connections with the Viking heritage of the islands. The festival involves a torch-light procession through the streets of Lerwick, led by the ceremonial chief, known as the Geiser Jarl. The highlight of the festivities is the burning of a replica Viking longship, which is associated with the Viking tradition of placing their dead chieftain in a longship before setting fire to it to ensure his safe arrival in Valhalla.

Lerwick's solid stone buildings are mirrored in the sheltered waters of the old harbour

LERWICK Map ref HU4741

Lerwick is the capital of Shetland and it is all because of fish. In the 17th century the sailing ships of the Dutch herring fleet found a safe haven in the waters of Bressay Sound, and trade with the crews brought prosperity to the Shetlanders. As more people came to capitalise on that trade, the settlement at Lerwick grew, stretching out along the coastline – the town's main thoroughfare, stone-flagged Commercial Street, still follows a tortuous winding route. This remains an area of great character and, as you wander, it is easy to imagine the hustle and bustle of those distant days. Look out for a local delicacy hanging in the butchers' windows – 'reestit mutton' is salt-cured, and gives a rich flavour to soups and stews. Another speciality is the knitwear – and nimble-fingered workers will even make you a garment to your own choice of pattern and colour.

The Dutch continued to have an effect on Lerwick down the years – the oldest building in the town is Fort Charlotte, its construction in the 1660s prompted by the Second Dutch War. It is roughly pentagonal in shape, with a battery overlooking Bressay Sound, set behind a zigzagged parapet. The fort saw no action, although in 1673 the garrison block was burnt by the Dutch, by now into their third war. It was only in 1780, when Britain was at loggerheads with Spain, France and the various states of Northern Europe, that the fort was finally completed and named Fort Charlotte after George III's

A supply ship in Lerwick harbour, which is also a base for North Sea oil rigs

queen. More recent building now encroaches on every side, and it is difficult to appreciate the scale of the structure from outside, but it is nevertheless well worth a visit.

If you want to seek out earlier inhabitants, you should make your way to the Iron-Age Clickhimin Broch, itself standing on the site of an even earlier Bronze-Age settlement, a mile (1.6km) southwest of Lerwick. It was occupied for about 1,000 years, and remains include a partially demolished broch which still stands to a height of 17 feet (5.2m).

The small island of Bressay protects Lerwick Harbour, acting as a natural barrier to the easterly winds and creating one of the safest anchorages in northern Europe. There is a regular ferry link between Bressay and Lerwick, enabling many of the people who live there to commute daily to work on the larger island. Bressay was an important fish processing centre during the boom years of herring fishing, but after its collapse in the 1930s the various factories on the island closed. Today, fish related industries once more dominate the Shetland economy with huge processing factories around Lerwick taking much of the total European pelagic catch and exporting it to places such as Eastern Europe, Japan and Africa.

Shetland has a rich tradition of fiddle music – catch a session at the famous Lounge in Lerwick, or listen out for a performance by the lively youngsters of Shetland's Young Heritage.

NOSS NATIONAL NATURE RESERVE

The tiny island of Noss lies just to the east of Bressay and can be reached by a short boat trip across Noss Sound, where there is a good chance of seeing porpoises. There is a visitor centre and a waymarked walking route around the island, which is home to around 7,000 pairs of gannets, 6,000 pairs of fulmars, 7,000 pairs of kittiwakes and 40,000 pairs of guillemots, together with smaller numbers of razorbills, puffins, black guillemots and shags. The island consists mainly of moorland, covered with heather and crowberry, among which you will find heath spotted orchids, tormentil and thrift; spring squill grows along the cliff tops.

VIKING LAW

In Viking Shetland there were a number of districts, each with its own parliamentary assembly, or 'ting', which met to decide matters of ownership and settle minor disputes. These districts live on to this day in the names of some of the current parishes – Aithsting, Nesting, Delting and so on. Once a year representatives of these tings met at Law Ting Holm, once a tiny islet at the north end of Tingwall Loch, reached by a narrow causeway which can still be traced in the boggy ground. Here they would resolve any weightier matters and pass new laws. Similar systems were introduced in other areas, including the Western Isles and in the Isle of Man and Iceland, where the system survives to this day.

The harbour at Scalloway is dominated by the tower of the old castle

MOUSA AND SCALLOWAY

Mousa is a small, uninhabited island lying off the east coast of southern Shetland, and can be reached by a short boat trip from Sand Lodge Pier. It is a wonderful place to visit, not only for its superb wildlife – the island is designated a Site of Special Scientific Interest – but also for its broch dating from around 100 BC to AD 300, which is widely acclaimed as the best preserved anywhere. At its base it is 50 feet (15.2m) in diameter, the walls are 43.5 feet (12.2m) high, and it has the typical twin-walled construction with an internal staircase. It is mentioned in *The Orkneyinga Saga* – Earl Harald arrived at 'Moseyjarborg' intent on battle with Erlund, who had abducted his mother, but the thought of trying to attack the broch quelled his ardour for a fight and the dispute was resolved by negotiation. Today the only squabbles are between neighbouring pairs of storm petrels, the smallest of Britain's seabirds, which nest in the holes in the walls.

Further up the long finger of southern Shetland, Scalloway was the medieval capital of the islands, and although today the seat of power has moved to Lerwick, it is still a town of notable importance. It lies at the centre of an historic area, with Tingwall, the centre of Norse administration, and the Loch of Strom, site of the ruins of the oldest castle in Shetland. Dominating the town is the spectacular ruined castle, built in 1600 by Earl Patrick Stewart but only inhabited for a few years before he and his son were executed in Edinburgh in 1615. Around 1640 it was occupied by a garrison of Cromwell's troops before falling into disrepair.

MUCKLE FLUGGA AND UNST

The name Muckle Flugga means 'big bird rock', and although many claim it is the most northerly scrap of the UK, just beyond it, to the north, lies Out Stack, to which this accolade truly belongs. The lighthouse on Muckle Flugga, which has helped steer boats around the northern tip of Shetland for over 100 years, was designed by Thomas Stevenson, the father of Robert Louis Stevenson, and completed in 1858. It is best viewed either at Saxa Vord or from Hermaness National Nature Reserve – and if you are lucky, you may also see, on a calm day, dolphins, porpoises or even killer whales breaking the surface of the water.

A ferry connects Unst with Yell and there is also an air service to the island. From Belmont, where the ferry docks, the road heads north passing the ruins of Muness Castle, the most northerly castle in Britain, and on towards Baltasound on the east side of the island. It was one of the principal herring fishing centres in Shetland between the 1880s and 1920s. Continuing north the road leads to Haroldswick with its pillar-box red Post Office, which is the most northerly in the British isles. There is an inescapable feeling of being on the edge of the world. Hermaness National Nature Reserve, in the northwest corner of Unst, is a brilliant gem in the treasure trove of Shetland wildlife sites. The cliffs, which rise to nearly 558 feet (170m), are home in summer to over 100,000 seabirds and the perpetual motion and continuous cacophony of sound with the backdrop of the North Atlantic offers a truly unique wildlife experience.

LIFE AT THE EDGE

The visitor centre at Hermaness National Nature Reserve is housed in the former lighthouse shore station, which was home to the families of the lighthouse-men of Muckle Flugga. It is run by Scottish Natural Heritage and offers an innovative introduction to the wildness of the landscape, the birds and the other wildlife of the reserve. The seabird cliffs themselves, set amidst a stunning maelstrom of wheeling gannets, fulmars and other species, are thick with patrolling puffins, so unused to visitors they are unafraid and you can sit undisturbed among them. An hour or so's moorland walk leads to these cliffs, during which time you are liable to be harmlessly dive-bombed by pairs of great skua, the Shetland 'bonxie'.

The lighthouse at Muckle Flugga, on its exposed rock

BLACK GOLD

Shetland history has always been inextricably linked to the sea – the Vikings arrived by sea to conquer and transform the land; fishing has always been important to the Shetland way of life – but nothing could match the discovery of North Sea oil for its impact on the islands. Sullom Voe is now the largest oil and gas terminal in Europe, its deep and sheltered waters providing a safe anchorage for the great supertankers which transport the crude oil all around the world. The oil gets to Sullom Voe by undersea pipeline, and the terminal handles on average 750,000 barrels per day. Oil revenues have given Shetland new and improved roads, a new fleet of inter-island ferries and many new community centres and other public facilities.

An upturned boat provides an unusual roof on the island of Yell

WHALSAY AND YELL

Whalsay, 5 miles (8km) long and 2 miles (3.2km) wide, lies 3 miles (4.8km) east of the Shetland mainland, and its name is derived from the Old Norse, *Ivals-ey*, 'whale's island', probably because of its shape. Much on Whalsay, with a population of 1,000, seems typical of Shetland as a whole, with fishing, crofting and peat-cutting in summer for winter fuel. But Whalsay is Shetland's most thriving fishing community, with a modern fishing fleet and a state-of-the-art harbour at Symbister. Oil revenue helped pay for the investment which will profit the community long after the oil has dried up.

There is evidence of human occupation stretching back to the third millennium BC, best displayed at Pettigarth's Field, comprising two houses, Bennie Hoose and Standing Stones of Yoxie. The 17th-century Pier House at Symbister, a restored Hanseatic Böd, is a small two-storey building at the end of its own jetty, which served as both home and store. It has its own windlass, used to unload alcohol, tobacco, cloth and salt from German ships in return for dried and salted fish.

Yell is the second largest island in the Shetland archipelago. It gets its name from the Old Norse, *geldr*, meaning 'barren', and the description is still apt. At Gloup is an old fishing station, one of the biggest in Shetland in the 19th century, which stands as a stark and poignant reminder of the rigours of a past times. The sixerns, local boats so called because they were crewed by six men, used to hunt cod and ling in the deep waters 40 miles (64.4km) offshore. Many men were lost to summer storms, and a memorial commemorates 58 men from 10 boats lost in 1881.

The Northern Isles

Leisure Information
Places of Interest
Shopping
Sports, Activities and the
Outdoors
Annual Events and Customs

Checklist

Leisure Information

TOURIST INFORMATION CENTRES

SHETLAND ISLANDS
Lerwick
The Market Cross. Tel: 01595 693434.

ORKNEY ISLANDS
Kirkwall
6 Broad Street. Tel: 01856 872856.
Stromness
Ferry Terminal Building, The Pier Head. Tel: 01856 850716.

OTHER INFORMATION

Ferries
Orkney Ferries, Shore Street, Kirkwall, Orkney. Tel: 01856 872044. Services throughout the islands.
P & O Scottish Ferries, Jamiesons Quay, Aberdeen. Tel: 01224 572615. Daily sailings to Orkney from Scrabster (Thurso). Sailings from Orkney (Stromness) to Shetland (Lerwick). Also sailings from Aberdeen.
Shetland Islands Council (Ferries). Tel: 01806 566259. Regular services throughout the islands.
Historic Scotland
Longmore House, Salisbury Place, Edinburgh. Tel: 0131 668 8800.

National Trust for Scotland
28 Charlotte Square, Edinburgh. Tel: 0131 243 9300. www.nts.org.uk
RSPB
Dunedin House, 25 Ravelston Terrace, Edinburgh. Tel: 0131 311 6500. www.rspb.com
Scottish Tourist Board
23 Ravelston Terrace, Edinburgh. Tel: 0131 332 2433. www.visitscotland.com
Scottish Wildlife Trust
Cramond House, Cramond Glebe Road. Edinburgh. Tel: 0131 312 7765. www.swt.org.uk
Weather
Weathercall for northwest Scotland. Tel: 09068 232795.

ORDNANCE SURVEY MAPS

Landranger 1:50,000 sheets 1, 2, 3, 4, 5, 6, 7, 18.

Places of Interest

There will be an admission charge at the following places of interest unless otherwise stated.
ORKNEY ISLANDS
BURRAY
Orkney Fossil and Vintage Centre
Viewforth, Burray. Tel: 01856 731255. Open May–Oct, daily.

HOY
Dwarfie Stane
Tel: 0131 668 8800. Open all reasonable times. Free.
Martello Tower
Hackness South Walls. Tel: 0131 668 8800.
Scapa Flow Visitor Centre
Lyness. Tel: 01856 791300. Open all year, closed winter weekends.

MAINLAND
Brough of Birsay
Eleven miles (17.7km) north of Stromness. Tel: 0131 668 8800. Accessible only at low tide. Norse settlement, Romanesque church, replica of Pictish sculptured stone (original is in the Museum of Antiquities, Edinburgh). Open mid-Jun to Sep, depending on tides. Free.
Click Mill
Dounby. Tel: 0131 668 8800. Open all reasonable times. Free.
Corrigal Farm Museum
Harray. Tel: 01856 771411. A 19th-century farmhouse and steadingwith displays of traditional building methods. There is also a barn kiln, a parish weaver's loom and traditional craffts. Open Mar–Oct, daily.
Earl Patrick's Palace
Kirkwall. Tel: 01856 871918/0131 668 8800. Open Apr–Sep daily.

Earl's Palace
Birsay. 11 miles (17.7km) north of Stromness. Tel: 0131 668 8800. Open Apr–Sep daily.

Kirbuster Farm Museum
Birsay. Tel: 01856 771268. Traditional rural dwelling. Open Mar–Oct, daily.

Maes Howe Chambered Cairn
Off the A965, west of Kirkwall. Tel: 0131 668 8800. Open all year, most days.

Orkney Natural and Maritime History Museum
52 Alfred Street, Stromness. Tel: 01856 850025. Open all year daily; closed Sun Mar–Oct, Christmas, New Year and 3 weeks in Feb/Mar.

Pier Arts Centre
Victoria Street, Stromness. Tel: 01856 850209. Open all year Tue–Sat. Free.

Rennibister Earth House
On A965, northwest of Kirkwall. Tel: 0131 668 8800. Open at all reasonable times. Free.

Skara Brae
Dounby. Six miles (9.7km) north of Stromness. Tel: 0131 668 8800. Open all year daily.

Stenness Standing Stones
Five miles (8km) northeast of Stromness. Tel: 0131 688 8800. Always open. Free.

Tankerness House
Broad Street, Kirkwall. Tel: 01856 873191. Open all year most days.

PAPA WESTRAY
Knap of Howar
On west side of Island. Tel: 0131 668 8800. A pair of 5,000-year-old buildings (one of the oldest sites in Europe),

Skara Brae was exposed during a fierce storm in 1850

yielding whalebone artefacts and stone borers and grinders. Free. Contact Orkney Ferries at Kirkwall. Tel: 01856 872044.

ROUSAY
Midhowe Broch and Cairns
On the west coast, on a promontory cut off by a deep rock-cut ditch. Tel: 0131 668 8800. An Iron-Age broch and walled enclosure. Also Midhowe Stalled Cairn, 'an elongated ship of death'. Open all reasonable times. Free.

SANDAY
Quoyness Chambered Tomb
On south coast, on the east side of Els Ness. Tel: 0131 668 8800. Open at all times. Free.

SOUTH RONALDSAY
Tomb of the Eagles and Bronze-Age House
Liddle Farm, St Margaret's Hope. Tel: 01856 831339. Open all year daily.

WESTRAY
Noltland Castle
Tel: 0131 668 8800. Open at all reasonable times. Free.

FAIR ISLE
Fair Isle Bird Observatory
Charter flights or mailboat sailings (twice weekly) from Shetland. Tel: 01595 760258. Open Apr–Oct.

SHETLAND ISLANDS
MAINLAND
Fort Charlotte
Lerwick. Tel: 0131 668 8800. Open any reasonable time. Free.
Jarlshof Prehistoric Site
nr Sumburgh Airport. Tel: 01950 460112. Open Apr–Sep daily.
Scalloway Castle
Tel: 0131 668 8800. Always open. Key on request from Shetland Woollen Co, Castle Street; from Royal Hotel on Sun.
Scalloway Museum
Main Street, Scalloway. Extensive displays of local artefacts and old photographs. Summer only.
Shetland Croft House Museum
Tel: 01595 695057. Open

May–Sep. Free.
Shetland Museum
Lower Hillhead, Lerwick. Tel: 01595 695057. Open all year most days. Free.
Up Helly Aa Exhibition
St Sunniva Street, Lerwick. Photographs of January Fire Festival and Viking longship.

MOUSA
Mousa Broch
Tel: 0131 668 8800 (01950 431367 to book boat trip from Sandwick). Always open. Free.

UNST
Muness Castle
Southeast corner of Unst. Tel: 0131 668 8800. Open all reasonable times (apply to key keeper). Free.

YELL
Old Haa Museum
Burravoe. Tel: 01957 722339. Open end Apr–Sep certain days. Free.

Shopping

LOCAL SPECIALITIES
ORKNEY ISLANDS
Distillery
Highland Park Distillery, Holm Road, on A961 near Kirkwall, Mainland. Open: shop all year, telephone for times of tours. Tel: 01856 874619.

Sports, Activities and the Outdoors

ANGLING
There are ample opportunities for angling of all kinds. Enquire at Tourist Information Offices.

BOAT TRIPS
SHETLAND ISLANDS
Dim River
Lerwick Harbour, Mainland. Trips in a Viking longship. Contact Tourist Information Centre.
Tel: 01595 693434.

CYCLE HIRE
ORKNEY ISLANDS
Orkney Cycle Hire, 54 Dundas Street, Stromness. Tel: 01856 850255.

GOLF COURSES
ORKNEY ISLANDS
The Orkney Golf Club, Grainbank, Kirkwall. Tel: 01856 872457.
Stromness Golf Club. Tel: 01856 850772.
SHETLAND ISLANDS
Shetland Golf Club, Dale. Tel: 01595 840369.

GUIDED TOURS
SHETLAND ISLANDS
Shetland Wildlife Tours. Longhill, Maywick. Tel: 01950 422483.

NATURE RESERVES
ORKNEY ISLANDS
Marwick Head Nature Reserve, Mainland. (RSPB). North from Marwick Bay. Tel: 01856 850176/0131 311 6500.
Hoy Nature Reserve, Hoy. (RSPB). Reached by boat from Stromness. Access at all times. Tel: 01856 791298/ 0131 311 6500.

SHETLAND ISLANDS
Hermaness National Nature Reserve, Unst. North end of island. Tel: 01957 711278. Open Apr–Sep.
Noss Nature Reserve, Isle of Noss. Tel: 01595 693345. Access by inflatable boat. Open mid-May to Aug. Charge.

WATERSPORTS
ORKNEY ISLANDS
Skolla Diving Centre, Gulberwick. Tel: 01595 694175.

Annual Events and Customs

ORKNEY ISLANDS
Kirkwall
Ba' Games. Held on 25th December and 1st January.
Stromness
Orkney Traditional Folk Festival. Late May.
St Magnus Festival. Major British Music Festival, late June.
SHETLAND ISLANDS
Lerwick
Up Helly Aa, late January–early February.
Other local Up Helly Aa during February and March throughout Shetland.

Atlas and Map Symbols

THE NATIONAL GRID SYSTEM

The National Grid system covers Great Britain with an imaginary network of 100 kilometre grid squares. Each square is given a unique alphabetic reference as shown in the diagram. These squares are sub-divided into one hundred 10 kilometre squares, each numbered from 0 to 9 in an easterly (left to right) direction and northerly (upwards) direction from the bottom left corner. Each 10 km square is similarly sub-divided into one hundred 1 km squares.

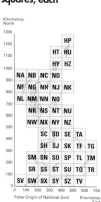

KEY TO ATLAS

MOTORWAY		A ROAD	
M4	Motorway with number	A1123	Other A road single/dual carriageway
Fleet	Motorway service area	╞═════╡	Road tunnel
	Motorway junction with and without number	Toll	Toll
3	Restricted motorway junctions		Road under construction
	Motorway and junction under construction		Roundabout
PRIMARY ROUTE		**B ROAD**	
A3	Primary route single/dual carriageway	B2070	B road single/dual carriageway
Grantham North	Primary route service area		B road interchange junction
BATH	Primary route destinations		B road roundabout with adjoining unclassified road
	Roundabout	→	Steep gradient
5	Distance in miles between symbols		Unclassified road single/dual carriageway
	Narrow Primary route with passing places	—○—╳—	Railway station and level crossing

KEY TO ATLAS

⌂	Abbey, cathedral or priory	-----	National trail
🐟	Aquarium	NT	National Trust property
♜	Castle	NTS	National Trust for Scotland property
⌒	Cave	🦭	Nature reserve
🌳	Country park	★	Other place of interest
🏏	County cricket ground	P+R	Park and Ride location
🐄	Farm or animal centre	♣	Picnic site
··········	Forest drive	🚂	Steam centre
❄	Garden	🎿	Ski slope natural
⛳	Golf course	🎿	Ski slope artifical
🏛	Historic house	ℹ	Tourist Information Centre
🐎	Horse racing	☀	Viewpoint
🏁	Motor racing	V	Visitor or heritage centre
🏛	Museum	🦒	Zoological or wildlife collection
☎	AA telephone		Forest Park
⊕	Airport	····	Heritage coast
Ⓗ	Heliport		National Park (England & Wales)
✗	Windmill		National Scenic Area (Scotland)

KEY TO TOURS

🚗	Tour start point	Buckland Abbey	Highlighted point of interest
➡	Direction of tour		
▫▫╌╎▫▫	Optional detour	⤻	Featured tour

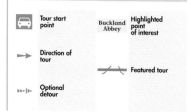

KEY TO WALKS

Scale 1:25,000, 2½ inches to 1 mile, 4cm to 1 km

	Start of walk		Line of walk
	Direction of walk	⊩⊩⊩	Optional detour
		Buckland Abbey	Highlighted point of interest

ROADS AND PATHS

M1 or A6(M)	M1 or A6(M)	Motorway
A 31(T) or A35	A 31(T) or A35	Trunk or main road
B 3074	B 3074	Secondary road
A 35	A 35	Dual carriageway
		Road generally more than 4m wide
		Road generally less than 4m wide
		Other road, drive or track
....		Path

Unfenced roads and tracks are shown by pecked lines

RAILWAYS

	Multiple track	Standard gauge	Embankment
	Single track		Tunnel
	Narrow gauge		Road over; road under
	Siding		Level crossing
	Cutting		Station

PUBLIC RIGHTS OF WAY

Public rights of way may not be evident on the ground

- - - -	Public paths	footpath	Byway open to all traffic
– – – –		bridleway	Road used as a public path
- - - -	Permissive path		Named path
– – – –	Permissive bridleway	Pennine Way	National trail or recreational path

The representation on this map of any other road, track or path is no evidence of the existence of a right of way

RELIEF

50 ·	Heights determined by	Ground survey
285 ·		Air survey

Contours are at 5 and 10 metres vertical interval

SYMBOLS

	Place of worship	with tower	○ W, Spr Well, Spring
		with spire, minaret or dome	Gravel pit
+		without such additions	
	Building		Other pit or quarry
	Important building		Sand pit
. T; A; R	Telephone: public; AA; RAC		
pylon pole	Electricity transmission line		Refuse or slag heap
△ △	Triangulation pillar		County Boundary (England & Wales)
	Bus or coach station		Water
⚲ ⚲	Lighthouse; beacon		Sand; sand & shingle
	Site of antiquity		National Park boundary
NT	National Trust always open		
FC	Forestry Commission		Mud

DANGER AREA
Firing and test ranges in the area
Danger!
Observe warning notices

VEGETATION

Limits of vegetation are defined by positioning of the symbols but may be delineated also by pecks or dots

	Coniferous trees		Non-coniferous trees
	Orchard		Heath
	Coppice		Marsh, reeds, saltings.

TOURIST AND LEISURE INFORMATION

	Camp site	PC	Public convenience
	Information centre	P	Parking
	Information centre (seasonal)		Viewpoint
	Caravan site	⊕	Mountain rescue post
	Picnic site		

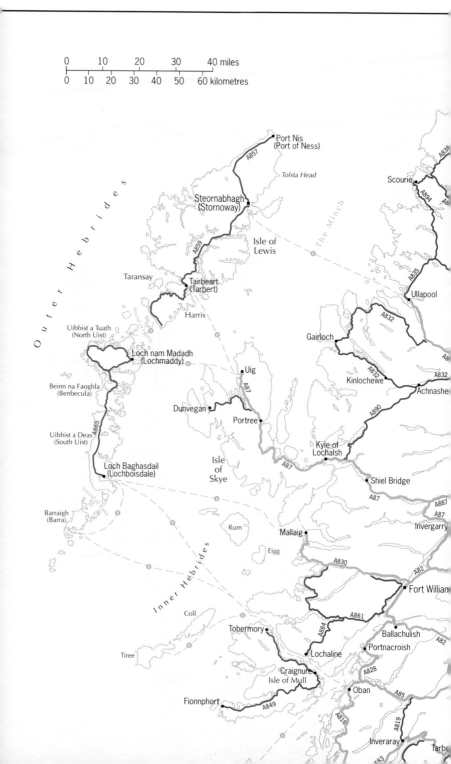

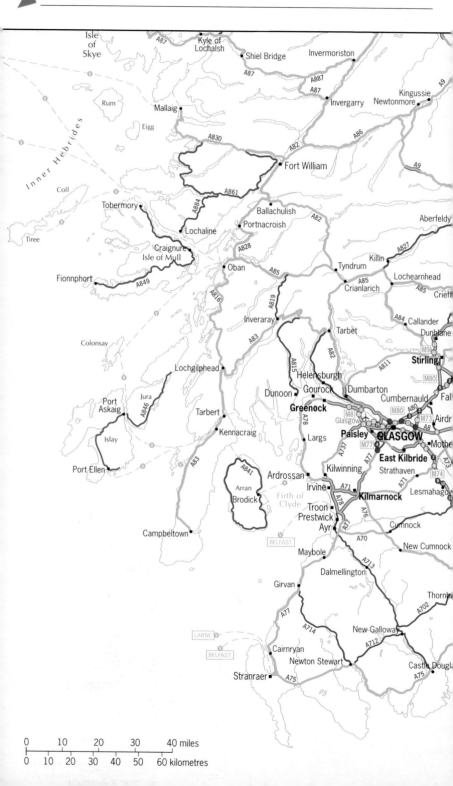

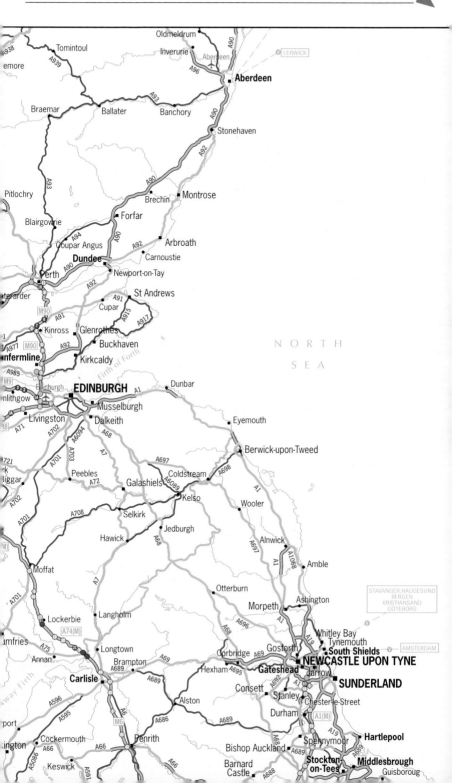

Index

Acknowledgements

The authors would like to thank the staff of the various Tourist Information Offices throughout the Highlands and Islands of Scotland, the Scottish Tourist Board, the National Trust for Scotland, and Caledonian MacBrayne Ferries for their invaluable assistance.

Third edition verified by Outcrop Publishing Services Ltd, Cumbria.

The Automobile Association wishes to thank the following photographers & libraries for their assistance in the preparation of this book.

D HARDLEY 13, 15, 17
THE MANSELL COLLECTION LTD 7e
NATURE PHOTOGRAPHERS LTD 6a (C Mylne)
SPECTRUM COLOUR LIBRARY 108, 115
CHARLES TAIT 104, 109, 111

All remaining pictures are held in the Association's own library (AA PHOTO LIBRARY) and were taken by J HENDERSON with the exception of the following pages 21 (A Baker), 3b, 9c, 10a, 11a, 11b, 68a, 72, 80, 85 (J Beazley), 20 (J Carnie), 32a, (S L Day), 3f, 7c, 7f, 9a, 10b, 10c, 68b, 81, 86, 102, 103, 105, 106, 107, 110, 112, 113, 114, 116, 118 (E Ellington), 6c, 7g, 8/9, 8c, 22, 32b, 62, 63, 64, 65, 79 (R G Elliott), 3e, 12a, (D Forss), 11c, 14, 16, 18, 56 (D Hardley), 6d (P Sharp), 89, 95, 96, 98 (M Taylor), 7d, 8a, 9b (R Weir), 3c (H Williams)